Family Book

The Table of the LORD

A First Eucharist Preparation Program

Gaynell Bordes Cronin

Ave Maria Press • Notre Dame, Indiana 46556

Excerpts from the English translation of *Rite of Baptism for Children* © 1969, International Committee on English in the Liturgy, Inc. (ICEL); excerpts from the English translation of *The Roman Missal* © 1973, ICEL. All rights reserved.

Excerpts from SHARING THE LIGHT OF FAITH, National Catechetical Directory for Catholics of the United States, copyright © 1979, by the United States Catholic Conference, Department of Education, Washington, DC, are used by permission of the copyright owner. All rights reserved.

Scripture quotations are taken from the *Good News Bible:* Copyright © American Bible Society 1976. Used with permission. For the United Kingdom, permission granted by the British and Foreign Bible Society and Collins Publishers, London.

Nihil Obstat: James T. O'Connor, S.T.D.
              Censor Librorum

Imprimatur: +Joseph T. O'Keefe, D.D.
              Vicar-General, Archdiocese of New York

The nihil obstat and imprimatur are official declarations that a book or pamphlet is free of doctrinal or moral error. No implication is contained therein that those who have granted the nihil obstat and imprimatur agree with the contents, opinions or statements expressed.

Copyright © 1986 Ave Maria Press, Notre Dame, Indiana 46556

All rights reserved. No portion of this book may be reproduced in any form, or by any means, without the written permission of the publisher.

International Standard Book Number: 0-87793-326-X

Library of Congress Catalog Card Number: 86-70131

Photography:
    Carolyn A. McKeone, 4, 18, 48; Joanne Meldrum, 20, 28; Patrick Mooney, 20; Gene Plaisted, 80; Religious News Service, 95; James L. Shaffer, 4, 36, 56, 64, 72, 88.

Art by Stephanie Cunningham

Printed and bound in the United States of America.

Acknowledgments

Growing in our faith is a family affair, an affair that is shared at our parish table of the Lord and our home table of the Lord. To the families and teachers in the parish of Holy Name of Mary, Croton-on-Hudson, New York, in Holy Name of Jesus parish, Valhalla, New York, and in the parish of St. Theresa, Briarcliff, New York, thank you. You welcomed and lived separate aspects of this program long before it was placed in print. It is your lived faith that is shared in these pages.

And for the people who gather at our home table of the Lord, the Cronin, Bordes, and Evans families, thank you. It is here that red beans and rice are served and we experience everyone and everything being made whole again. It is with the listening presence, encouragement and practical insights of Marlene Liede and the guidance and sensitive direction of Joan Bellina that this program and journey of faith is shared.

— Gaynell Bordes Cronin

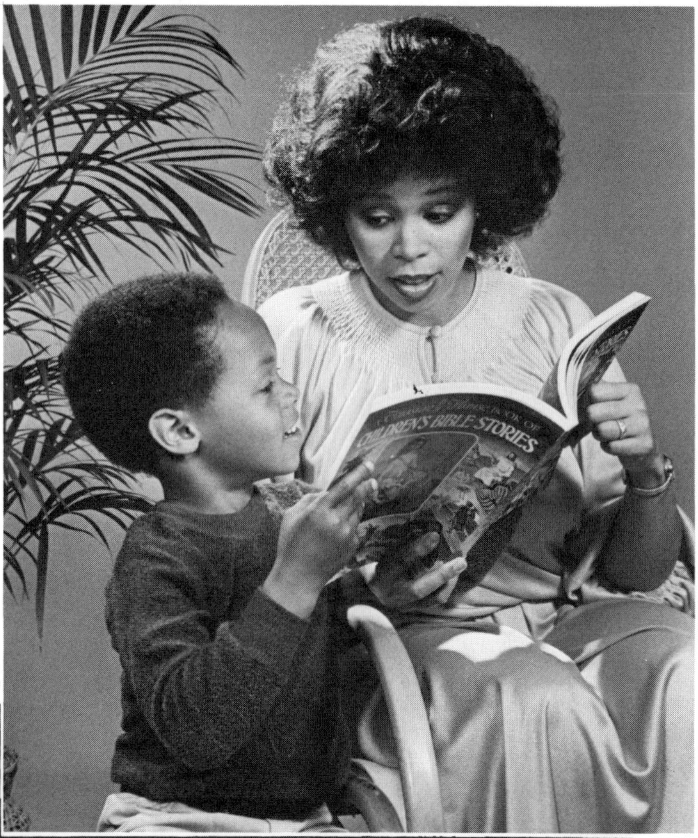
CHILDREN'S BIBLE STORIES

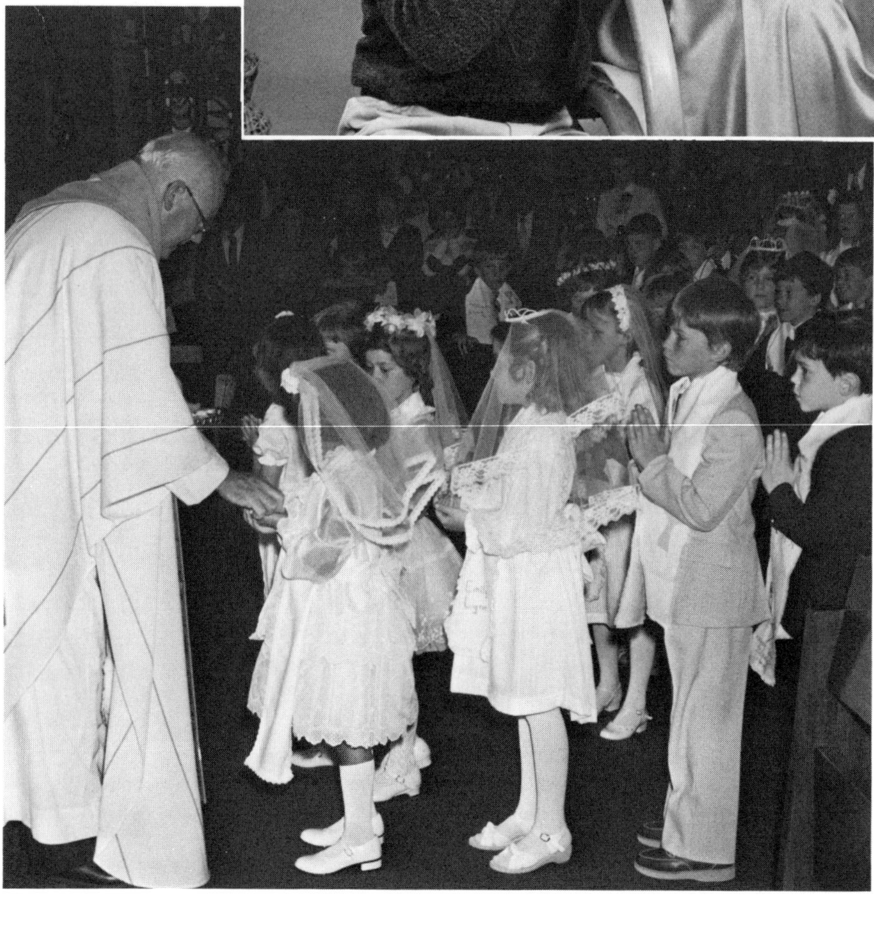

Table of Contents

Introduction 6
Parents as Educators 7

How to Use *The Table of the Lord*
    Structure of the *Child's Book* 9
    Structure of the *Family Book* 10
    Family Growth Experiences 13
    Family Prayer 13
    The *Jesus Tree* 14
    The Parish and the Family Together 16
    Evaluating Faith Growth 16
    Where Do We Begin? 17

Teaching the *Child's Book*
    Unit 1 The Wedding at Cana (Celebrating) 21
    Unit 2 Zacchaeus (Forgiving) 29
    Unit 3 The Good Samaritan (Listening) 37
    Unit 4 The Daughter of Jairus (Caring) 43
    Unit 5 Martha and Mary (Giving) 49
    Unit 6 Jesus Feeds the 5,000 (Sharing) 57
    Unit 7 The Last Supper (Remembering) 65
    Unit 8 The Breakfast at the Lake (Belonging) 73
    Unit 9 The Road to Emmaus (Receiving) 81
    Unit 10 Jesus in Others (Serving) 89

Introduction

Every Sunday we were invited to my grandmother's home. At her table we gathered with aunts, uncles and cousins, for a red beans and rice dinner as we shared the experiences of our week.

It was around my grandmother's table that stories were told, dreams shared, disappointments revealed, hopes renewed. This was family! We knew that it would be there through the good times and bad times. And when we left her house, we left with a sense of belonging, of remembering who we were, and of being recommitted to where we were going together.

My childhood Sunday memory of going to Mass and going to my grandmother's home is one in my mind. On both of these occasions we gathered with friends at the table of the Lord. To both of these tables we brought our experiences, and from both we went forth to live as family with and for others.

In our homes, we live as family. To the table where we gather for meals we bring all the experiences of our day—pains, burdens, heartaches, joys and delights. We bless, encourage, forgive, affirm, accept and love. Through sharing a meal with one another, we celebrate life. At this table we know the presence of God through each person.

This is our home table of the Lord.

And where does the heart of family living as a parish take place? It is at the altar where we gather every Sunday as the family of God to celebrate the Eucharist. To this table too we bring all our experiences; from this table we go forth to become a self-gift to others. Through sharing a meal with one another, we celebrate the life of Jesus.

This is our parish table of the Lord.

We prepare our children to receive and live the Eucharist as family at our home table of the Lord and as community at our parish table of the Lord. And we deepen our understanding and appreciation of the Eucharist in our own lives.

Parents as Educators

Popes and bishops have referred to our homes as the domestic church. As such, we are encouraged to provide a nurturing environment where the seeds of faith can take root and grow and to share our faith through family living.

As domestic church we pass on our faith through word and deed to our children. What dignity is ours! The handing on of the good news from person to person, the transmitting of our personal experience of faith, is the heart of encountering the living God.

As domestic church we discover that our homes are sacred and that family members are holy. As domestic church we light family candles, break bread together, bless one another, welcome the stranger, admit wrongs, forgive injuries, care for the sick, show compassion, celebrate the gift of life. We share our faith through the primary relationships we have in our family and through the human actions of daily living. In these relationships and actions we help our children recognize the presence of God.

Since the child's immediate environment, normally the home, remains the principal setting in which children experience a relationship with God, the main work of sacramental preparation belongs in the home. We have a rich heritage to pass on to our children. Through our daily family actions we share our Christian faith in an informal way. While a specific program for sacrament preparation is necessary, it should merely provide structure and explanation for an experience that our children have every day—living as part of a faith-filled family. It is that experience that provides the foundation for our children's development as Christians.

The Table of the Lord will help us articulate and demonstrate our own faith for our child as we prepare together for his or her First Communion. Guidelines from the *National Catechetical Directory* offer us an understanding of the thinking ability of our second grader:

> Children around the age of seven tend to think concretely; they grasp concepts like "unity" and "belonging" from experiences such as sharing, listening, eating, conversing, giving, thanking, and celebrating (No. 122).

Our children first experience these actions in the home. And through scripture stories, they can see the value Jesus placed on these actions in his own life. Through the celebration of the Eucharist children begin to recognize these same actions as the rites of the Mass.

> Such experiences coupled with explanations of the Eucharist adapted to their intellectual capacity and with future efforts to familiarize them with the main events of Jesus' life, help them to participate more meaningfully in the action of the Mass and to receive Christ's body and blood in Communion in an informed and reverent manner (No. 122).

We understand and appreciate life lived as a sacrament as we experience, even celebrate, the actions of family life, the Eucharist, and Jesus revealed to us through scripture.

The *National Catechetical Directory* stresses that

> Catechesis for First Communion is conducted separately from introductory catechesis for the Sacrament of Reconciliation, since each sacrament deserves its own concentrated preparation (No. 122).

Thus your child has already received instruction in the sacrament of reconciliation. Throughout this program you will be given opportunities for recognizing and experiencing ways we offer and receive forgiveness in our daily family living and as a community at Mass. Many of the family activities, as well as one of the community prayer services offered during this program, provide moments for forgiveness. All of these experiences help to deepen your child's appreciation and understanding of the sacrament of reconciliation.

As we prepare our children for First Communion, most of us feel the need for some review of the theology of Eucharist. This book addresses that need. Parents should also feel free to call on the person who is directing the sacramental preparation in their parish. The director has an overview of the whole program and is an important representative of the parish community which will welcome the children into fuller participation. Further, the director, on behalf of the parish community, will be offering additional activities related to the preparation of the children for First Communion. It is important that the children see the connection between the home community—the home table of the Lord—and the parish community—the parish table of the Lord.

How to Use
The Table of the Lord

The Table of the Lord consists of 10 units based on scripture that will help you prepare your child to receive First Communion.

Structure of the *Child's Book*

Each unit in this *Family Book* corresponds to a unit in the *Child's Book*. Each is centered on a theme which is shown in a specific action in family living, in the life of Jesus, and in a particular part of the Mass.

The theme, the scripture story used to illustrate it, and the part of the Mass introduced, are listed below:

Celebrating	The Wedding at Cana	Introductory Rite
Forgiving	Zacchaeus	Penitential Rite
Listening	The Good Samaritan	The Gospel
Caring	The Daughter of Jairus	General Intercession
Giving	Martha and Mary	Preparation of the Altar and the Gifts
Sharing	Jesus Feeds the 5,000	Eucharistic Prayer
Remembering	The Last Supper	Memorial Acclamation
Belonging	The Breakfast at the Lake	Sign of Peace
Receiving	The Road to Emmaus	Communion Rite
Serving	Jesus in Others	Concluding Rite

As you prepare to use this program, look at the *Child's Book* and review any one of the units in it to become familiar with its structure. You will find that each unit is divided into three parts: a retelling of a parable or story of Jesus, a "Prayer of Imagination," and a section called "Let's Talk About the Story" which contains discussions and activities.

Structure of the *Family Book*

The *Family Book* is made up of 10 units that will help you use and explain the 10 corresponding units in the *Child's Book*.

Each unit in this *Family Book* is divided into three sections:

REFLECTING	We reflect on the action of Jesus
	We reflect on the action of Eucharist
	We reflect on the action of family living
EXPERIENCING	We experience the action of Jesus
	We experience the action of Eucharist
	We experience the action of family living
PRAYING	We pray at the home table of the Lord

As you are ready to use each unit of this program, first read the unit in the *Child's Book*. The parable or story is adapted from scripture, so you may want to read it in a Bible as well so you can understand it more fully and be able to answer questions your child may have.

REFLECTING

After you have finished this, read through the "Reflecting" section of the unit in the *Family Book*. The short reflections direct attention to the action discussed in the unit as an action of Jesus, an action of Eucharist, and an action of family living.

EXPERIENCING

Then work on the "Experiencing" section as follows:

We Experience the Action of Jesus

A. Discuss the pictures with your child. Sample questions are provided as discussion starters. Typical answers are also given. These are merely examples of the ways some children respond to the questions—they are not *right or wrong*. Allow the discussion to develop naturally. Most children are eager to get to the story, so don't spend too much time on the picture; use it simply as an introduction.

B. Read the story to your child. Most children this age comprehend what they hear better than what they read. Unless your child asks to read the story to you, it is better for you to read it aloud. Your own personal warmth and frequent eye contact with your child will greatly enhance the telling of the story.

C. Pray the Prayer of Imagination. This is an introduction to meditative prayer that is appropriate to your child's age and experience. Most children enjoy this type of prayer. Read the sentences slowly with a pause for reflection after each. Usually the material given is enough, but if your child has difficulty with this type of prayer, you may want to add more specific questions. For example, the Prayer of Imagination for Lesson 1, The Wedding at Cana, concludes with three questions. You could expand on these questions:

What do you see?

What kind of room is it? What color? What are the people wearing? What kind of food is there?

What do you hear?

Is there music playing? Are the people talking? Is it quiet or noisy? Can you hear Mary? Jesus?

What do you feel?

Are you excited? happy? Are you glad to be at this party with your friends? Are you worried when you hear Mary say that there won't be enough wine to go around? How do you feel when Jesus takes care of the problem?

Again, be sensitive to your child. The prayer may vary in length depending on his or her attention span. Any time your child appears to be restless, break off without comment and go on to the next part of the lesson.

D. Responding to the story. This section uses phrases from the story you just read with your child to focus more clearly on the action which forms the theme of the lesson. Questions and typical responses are provided as discussion starters. Select a method for responding to the statement in the *Child's Book* that is appropriate for your child's ability and preferences. Here are some suggestions:

- your child may write his or her own answers
- your child may tell you his or her responses, and you write them in the spaces provided
- your child may draw a picture in response to a statement

- your child may cut pictures from magazines or use family snapshots and paste them in the space provided

Most parents and children prefer to mix all of the above suggestions in order to provide some variety in this section of the program.

> ***ONE CAUTION:*** Remember that this program is an opportunity for sharing your faith with your child. Listen to what your child says; be sensitive to his or her feelings and perceptions. ***Don't become distracted with spelling, grammar or other mechanical aspects of your child's response.***

E. An activity. Most of the lessons include an activity that relates to the theme of the lessons. These can be carried out as simply or as elaborately as desired.

We Experience the Action of Eucharist

This section focuses on the celebration of the Eucharist. In each unit your child learns a response for a particular part of the Mass as you briefly explain it. Writing the priest's words or the congregation's response helps the child remember the words and recognize them during the eucharistic celebration.

We Experience the Action of Family Living

This section relates the theme of the lesson to our family life. While the focus is usually on the home, the child is also made aware of the parish family and the world family. Emphasis is on Jesus present in his people gathered together. Each unit includes a symbol which the child places on the family *Jesus Tree* (see the explanation of the Jesus Tree on pages 14-15 of this book).

Now you are ready for the "Praying" section:

PRAYING

We Pray at the Home Table of the Lord

Each unit concludes with a table prayer to be celebrated with the family. These prayers form an important part of the program.

They help the child see the connection between the home table and the parish table of the Lord. This interconnectedness is an important aspect of our understanding of Eucharist. Each table prayer uses a family candle, a family blessing cup, or a family tablecloth.

Most of the lessons offer optional activities that reinforce the theme. These activities can take place at any time after the presentation of the lesson, but are most effective if done soon.

Family Growth Experiences

The director of the program will distribute sheets containing Family Growth Experiences which spotlight particular actions of everyday family living. These actions correspond to the actions of Jesus presented in the scripture stories and to the actions of the parts of the Mass. Hopefully, our children will begin to recognize the similarities in these human actions.

By choosing to be together as a family, we speak clearly of the value and worth we place upon shared family experiences. Again, we want our children to begin to recognize God's presence in the actions of daily living and in the people who share that living. For it is through the ordinary actions of family life that we live the Eucharist.

It also is through the simple actions of everyday living that we choose to grow. Through these growth experiences we build self-esteem, recognize the gifts of others, offer moments of thankfulness, stand in awe of creation, reveal a basic stance that life is a gift to be celebrated. Through family living we develop with our children the skills of resolving conflicts, of forgiving, of healing, of listening to another with the heart.

Family Prayer

Prayer plays an important part throughout this program. In addition to the prayers contained in the scripture units and the *Child's Book,* the director of the program will distribute other prayers for the family. These prayers help us to remember God's presence in the ordinary actions of family living and to mark and ritualize his presence on special celebration days. Preparation for the Eucharist and living the life of the Eucharist is not something separate from daily living. Celebrating special moments and events as family is the foundation for understanding and appreciating the celebration of the Sunday Liturgy of the Eucharist as parish family.

Gestures are used in most of these family prayers. Sometimes our children forget that gestures are a form of prayer. Performed with meaning, a gesture can lift our spirits and renew us.

In the prayer services which end each unit you will be using a family candle, a family blessing cup, or a family tablecloth. (You will need a large candle, a goblet or cup, and a sheet.) The family candle and blessing cup are introduced in Unit 1, and the family tablecloth in Unit 5. Catechesis begins easily when we answer the questions our children ask us: Why are we lighting our family candle? Why are we using our blessing cup? Why is our family cloth on our table?

The *Jesus Tree*

The tree is a natural sign of life. Through family trees we remember our ancestors, those men and women from whom we have received life. Family trees tell the story of our heritage. In these stories family members discover their roots and are offered a sense of identity and belonging.

As we remember the lives of our ancestors through our family tree, we can remember the life of Jesus and our invitation to share in that life as the family of God through the *Jesus Tree*. Help your child copy the shape of the *Jesus Tree* (see page 15) onto a large piece of fabric or colored posterboard. Or your child can design his or her own shape for the *Jesus Tree*. Place the tree in the room where your family gathers for meals so that everyone in your family can see it daily. Be sure to print the words "JESUS TREE" prominently on it. After completing each scripture story, your child will be asked at the family meal to place a sign for that story on the *Jesus Tree*. Sample signs are found in the "We Experience the Action of Family Living" section of each chapter of this book. Children can copy these for the *Jesus Tree* or create symbols of their own.

Our children learn, celebrate, and express their experiences of life through signs and symbols. Children are delighted to be able to review the stories of Jesus through these signs. The *Jesus Tree* with its signs becomes a daily reminder of the way Jesus lived his life in the care and love of others and of our call to do the same.

Since we share in the life of Jesus as brothers and sisters, we have roots and a common heritage. We are members of the family of God. After completing Unit 1, your child will be asked to place the name of each family member on the *Jesus Tree* to show and remind them of their heritage. Rooted in Jesus we receive, live, and share his life with others as family.

Jesus Tree

How to Use *The Table of the Lord*

The Parish and the Family Together

Through baptism each of us was invited on a lifelong journey of faith as we were initiated and welcomed into the faith community. Sharing in the faith-filled life of the Christian community we began to live the good news of Jesus. The sacraments of Eucharist and confirmation will be further steps in this lifelong conversion. The entire Christian community shares in the responsibility of sponsorship in these three sacraments of initiation: baptism, Eucharist, confirmation.

Eucharist is the thanksgiving feast of a people who know they are deeply loved. The home and the parish both have distinctive roles in providing the environment for children to grow in oneness, a sign of the bread of the Eucharist, and to grow in gladness, a sign of the wine of the Eucharist as they give living witness to their faith.

Through education and celebration, our children are initiated into the eucharistic community by family, parish and school. (This program complements the formal religious education children receive in the parish school or center.) By worshipping with the family our children express what they have learned about the Eucharist and the life of Jesus; they celebrate what they have experienced at their home table of the Lord.

At the same time, the community's presence at your parish Sunday celebration of the Eucharist, coupled with their prayerful support, their understanding and living of the good news, encourages the faith growth of our children. Through three prayer services, a community meal, and a vigil the Christian community will witness its faith for our children.

Evaluating Faith Growth

As parents, we ask what our children should know and understand before they receive their First Communion. It is good for us to remember that First Communion is only one step in a lifelong process of learning to appreciate Jesus and the Eucharist. We want to provide the environment so that our children will be aware of some of the events in Jesus' life, be able to distinguish the eucharistic bread from ordinary table bread, and reflect a desire to receive the Eucharist. These are the basics our children should know and understand.

As this program is completed, we could ask ourselves the following questions in evaluating our child's readiness to receive the Eucharist:

Does our child have an awareness
- of God's love?
- of the call to serve others as Jesus did?
- of the gift of the Spirit?
- of the difference between ordinary bread we eat at home and the eucharistic bread?

Is our child beginning
- to experience the presence of Jesus in the action of daily family living?
- to know the life of Jesus through shared scripture stories?
- to participate more meaningfully in the actions of the Mass?
- to show a desire to receive the Eucharist?
- to experience the sense of unity and belonging which is the heart of the life of the Eucharist in the home family and parish family?
- to see the similarities between the home table of the Lord and the parish table of the Lord?
- to participate at home in living the life of the Eucharist by making a gift of self to others?

Where Do We Begin?

With a prayer, a hope, a dream, a smile, a thank you, we begin this journey of growing in our faith. Sharing that faith with others is really a simple thing, a thing of joy. We are all poets and philosophers of the heart; we are all seekers of the holy; we all try to live in the abundant goodness of God and see that goodness in others. Often, we fail. But we begin again. In the rhythm and actions of everyday living, we know God's presence. It is the recognition and living in that presence that we can share so beautifully with our children.

Before beginning the units in the *Child's Book,* spend a few moments with your child reading the Introduction to that book. Then, as your child signs his or her name on page 7 in the book, talk about his or her specialness; as you and your child write in the date, thank your child for being in your life. You may also want to talk about the *Jesus Tree* and help your child make one at this point.

Share with your child the joy you feel in beginning to know Jesus through stories and through praying together. Explain how excited the family is to have this opportunity to grow in its own understanding and appreciation of Jesus, the Eucharist, and the presence of God in family living, and in making this preparation for First Communion a family affair.

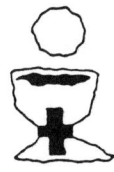

Teaching
The *Child's Book*

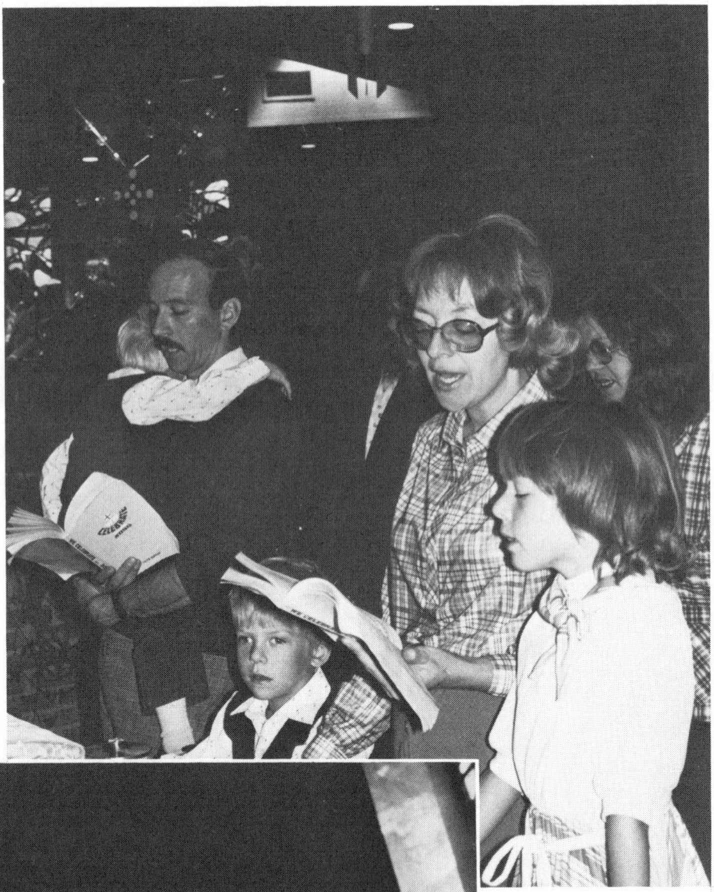

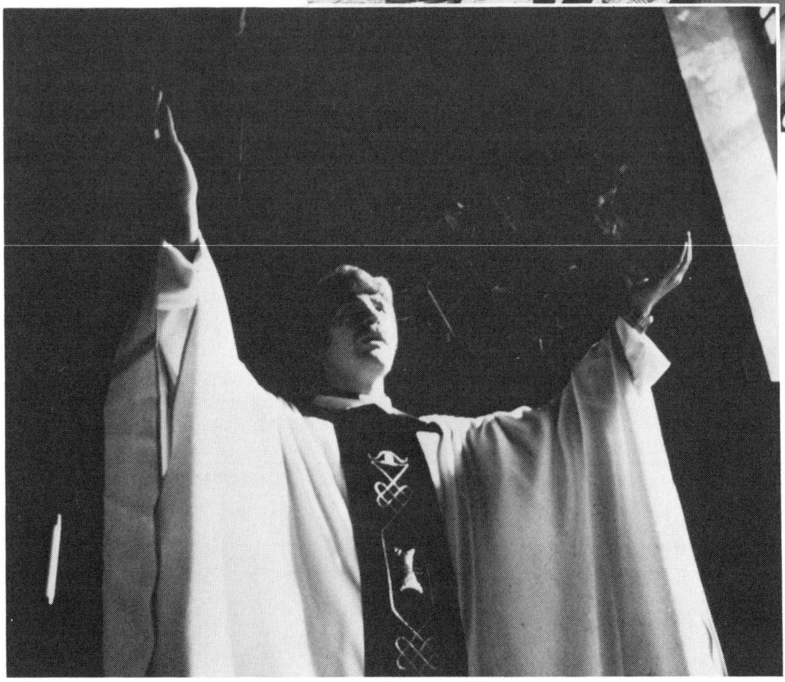

1 Celebrating

The Wedding at Cana

(John 2:1-12)

When we gather together as the family of God, we celebrate and praise God.

REFLECTING

We Reflect on the Action of Jesus

Jesus described the kingdom of God as a wedding feast, a great banquet rejoicing in the presence of God. In the story of the water made into wine, we have a sign of life in the kingdom, of the new life of the community. As God's people, we are called to a new life of gladness and joy; we are called to celebrate together.

At the wedding at Cana Jesus began his work by giving us a sign of the power, love and care of his Father. In this story the writer, John, wants us to think of the Eucharist. The changing of the water into wine is a sign of the sacrament of the Eucharist in which we experience God's love for us in Jesus. Since sacraments are actions of Jesus celebrated by the community, every time we gather for Eucharist, we partake in the life of Jesus. And we as church become visible as a community. As church, the family of God, we too are a sacrament. We allow the power, love and care of God to change our lives and, through the way we live, the lives of those around us. Like Mary, we are confident that Jesus will respond to our needs and the needs of others.

We Reflect on the Action of Eucharist

We gather to celebrate and worship as the family of God at Mass.

The Lord is present in the gathered assembly. As part of the Introductory Rite of the Mass, the entrance procession, song and greeting begin our liturgy and help us become a worshipping and celebrating community. This is the community which will welcome to the table of the Lord the children who are now preparing for first Eucharist. It is this community which will help our children grow in their faith and worship.

We Reflect on the Action of Family Living

As a family we celebrate birthdays, anniversaries, weddings, the beginning of school, forgiveness, the seasons, holidays, holy days. We have a deep need to celebrate. To our celebrations we bring all of our experiences of living. From our celebrations we return to everyday living with renewed hearts, refreshed spirits, and a sense of the significance of our lives.

The eucharistic celebration too brings us closer to one another, and to the Lord who is always with us. In the act of celebrating we become a community, praising and thanking God for all the gifts of creation, for the gift of one another, and for the gift of daily family living where we experience God's love and care for us.

EXPERIENCING

We Experience the Action of Jesus

A. Discuss the picture on page 11 of the *Child's Book* with your child.

> *How are these people celebrating?* (dancing, eating, playing music, talking, enjoying being together . . .)
>
> *How do you think these people feel?* (happy, welcomed, excited . . .)
>
> *Where is Jesus?* (by the jars, with Mary and the waiter . . .)
>
> *What is he doing?* (talking to the waiter, changing the water . . .)
>
> *Can you remember a time when you attended a similar celebration?*
>
> *How did you feel?*

B. Read the story to your child.

C. Pray the Prayer of Imagination at the end of the story.

D. Responding to the story: Remind your child that the words

"One day there was a wedding"

come from the story you just read. Give your child time to respond to the first statement in this section. As your child shares the words or pictures he or she has chosen, introduce the theme of celebrating. Besides your child's favorite day of celebration, recall days and times that the family celebrates during the year and the special foods, songs, prayers or actions associated with these celebrations. Help your child recognize that when we celebrate we come together to show how happy and thankful we feel about someone being in our life, about something that happened to us. In many celebrations we honor someone. Your birthday celebration honors you; a wedding anniversary honors a couple; a saint's day honors a good person; many of our country's holidays honor men, women or events that have shaped our history. At the celebration of the wedding at Cana, people honored a man and woman in marriage.

Ask your child:

How do you like to celebrate your favorite day?

Why do you celebrate this day?

Who is present at this celebration?

Is it more fun to celebrate alone or with others?

Point out that bringing people together is more important than the food or decorations. Talk about the people you enjoy being with for a celebration. As your child completes the second statement on page 15, ask why each person is important for this favorite day celebration.

As your child responds to the statements on page 16 under

"Jesus, his mother, and his friends were invited"

explain how much Jesus loved to celebrate, not only at weddings, but at different meals he ate with his friends and at worship celebrations at the temple. As Christians we mark Sunday as a special celebration day. Every Sunday we are invited to honor and praise God's care and love for us in Jesus by celebrating the meal of the Eucharist together. Celebrations bring people together.

Help your child see the similarities between people gathering for a celebration at home and for the celebration of the Mass. Point out the similarities in the actions performed at these celebrations (singing, eating, giving, receiving, telling stories . . .). The celebration of the Eucharist is an action that gathers the people of God together. To be invited to share this meal with friends is an honor.

Ask your child:

> *Who is present at our Sunday celebrations?* (family, friends, priest, others . . .)
>
> *Who leads the celebration?* (the priest)
>
> *What do we do in the celebration?* (sing, praise God, worship together, remember Jesus, listen . . .)
>
> *Why do we gather?* (we can thank and praise God together, we share the bread of life, Jesus asked us to remember him . . .)

You may want to talk about ways the family can make Sunday a special day.

E. Talk about how family members feel when they come together to celebrate. Explain to your child that just as you celebrate as family at home, so you also celebrate as the family of God every Sunday at Mass. We gather to praise and rejoice in God's presence among us. It is an honor to be invited to this celebration. Allow time for your child to complete the invitation on page 17.

We Experience the Action of Eucharist

A. Help your child complete the responses we say during the INTRODUCTORY RITE of the Eucharist on page 18.

B. The entrance procession at the beginning of Mass usually consists of ministers with lighted candles, a cross, a reader who may carry the gospel book, servers and the priest. We show our oneness as we stand and sing the entrance song. Then we make the sign of the cross. Signing with the cross was a gesture done by Christians as early as the second century. It is a form of self-blessing which reminds us that we were baptized in the name of the Father, Son and Holy Spirit.

The greeting offered by the presiding minister is one of the most ancient elements of the Introductory Rite. The priest welcomes us in the name of the Lord through one of three greetings which are simple statements of God's presence in our community. We show our union with God, the priest, and one another as we respond: "And also with you."

C. At the celebration of the Eucharist point out the INTRODUCTORY RITE to your child. Note the gestures of the priest as he welcomes us to this celebration.

We Experience the Action of Family Living

A. Have your child share with the family the invitation to attend Mass.

B. During the meal, ask your child to tell in his or her own words the story of THE WEDDING AT CANA. Discuss ways family members can thank and praise God together in celebration for what God has done and continues to do in our lives. Since Jesus is present in the people gathered, talk about the importance of all family members being present to celebrate the Eucharist. Be sure to thank your child for sharing.

C. Place a sign for THE WEDDING AT CANA on the *Jesus Tree*. (See the *Jesus Tree* instructions, pages 14-15 of this book. If you have not yet made your family *Jesus Tree,* do so now.)

The Wedding at Cana *(Celebrating)*

Blessing Cup

At Mass we gather at our parish table of the Lord to celebrate and give thanks for God's many blessings. As Jesus did at the table of the Last Supper, the celebrant invites us to share in the cup of blessing, the wine. Wine is a sign of gladness.

In our families we also give thanks for God's many blessings. Choose one cup or goblet as your blessing cup and place it in your kitchen. Use it for all celebrations: holidays, holy days, anniversaries, birthdays, any joyful events. Invite family members to bring the blessing cup to the family meal filled with their favorite beverage whenever they want the family to share in a blessing. At the end of the meal, the person raises the cup and gives thanks for his or her blessing. Then in silence the cup is passed around the table and each person drinks from it.

Being thankful as a family for God's many blessings in our daily family living is the foundation for celebrating the Eucharist as the family of God. We are blessed with God's presence in Jesus and in one another.

PRAYING AT OUR HOME TABLE OF THE LORD

Have each family member cut out a symbol for the Jesus Tree, and print his or her name on it. Place your family candle and the family blessing cup filled with wine or juice on the table.

Leader:	Welcome to our home table of the Lord celebration. In the name of the Father, and of the Son, and of the Holy Spirit.
All:	**Amen.**
Leader:	As we light our family candle, we remember all the times we have gathered to celebrate birthdays, anniversaries, holy days, holidays. We recall all the meals we have eaten around this table as family.

Light the family candle.

Leader: As we pass our blessing cup, we thank God for all the people in our family, _____*(name family members)*_____.
As each person drinks from the cup, thank God in your heart for that person.

Pass the family blessing cup.

Leader: As we place our names on the *Jesus Tree,* we remember that we are all members of Jesus' family and daily share in his life.

Place the names on the Jesus Tree.

Leader: Lord,
We thank you for being able to celebrate and eat meals together as family.
May we always enjoy your presence in one another.

The Lord be with you.

All: **And also with you.**

Offer one another a gesture of welcome and greeting.

The Wedding at Cana *(Celebrating)*

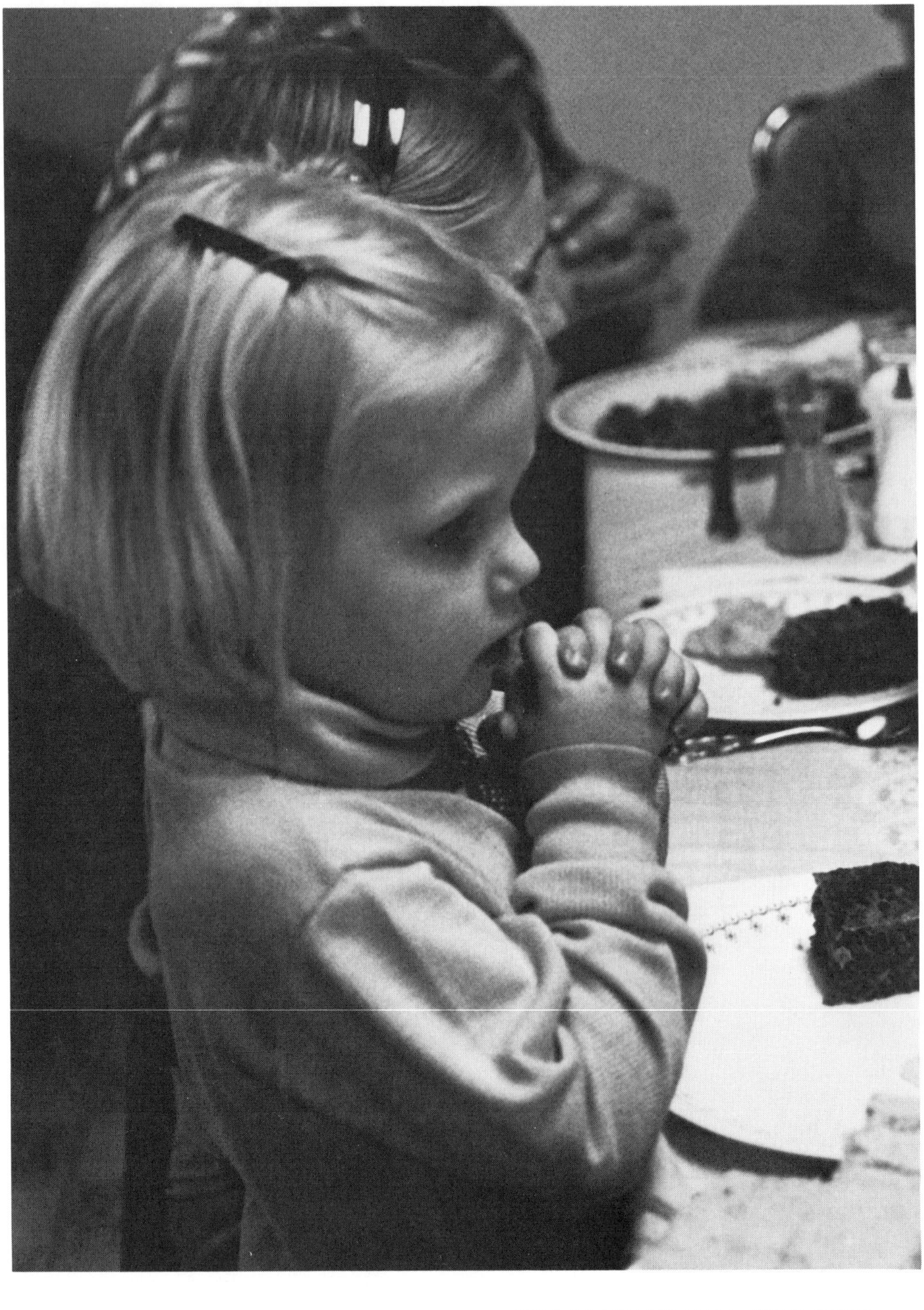

2 Forgiving

Zaccheus

(Luke 19:1-10)

The Eucharist helps us to forgive and to seek forgiveness, and to grow in love with God and one another.

REFLECTING

We Reflect on the Action of Jesus

In this story Luke offers us an example of repentance. Like the parables of the shepherd who searches for his lost sheep, the wife who tries to find her lost coin, and the father who reaches out to his lost son, Jesus seeks Zacchaeus.

Zacchaeus, like Matthew, was a tax collector, a social outcast. Curiosity impelled Zacchaeus to climb a tree to see Jesus, but then, touched by Jesus' love, acceptance and mercy, Zacchaeus undergoes a true change of heart. He eagerly offers to give half of his possessions to the poor and promises to repay fourfold anyone he has cheated.

In imitating Jesus, we offer love and acceptance to others so that they too can believe in God's love for them, the deep love of God that seeks our return, that longs to be welcomed into our homes and into our hearts.

We Reflect on the Action of Eucharist

The Eucharist itself is a sacrament of reconciliation, a celebration of our oneness with God and with one another. Before offering our gift at the altar, we participate in a Penitential Rite at the beginning of Mass. We pause to reflect on our failures to love. Then we proclaim our need for forgiveness and for reconciliation by saying the traditional *Confiteor* or responding "Lord, have mercy" to the invocations spoken by the priest.

We Reflect on the Action of Family Living

In our homes we have abundant opportunities to experience God's love through one another. We can call others to grow by our belief in them, by our acceptance of them. Love helps us to become whole persons, to take responsibility for our life as Zacchaeus did. As family, we practice the art of forgiveness. These family experiences of reconciliation prepare us to celebrate God's love in the sacraments of reconciliation and Eucharist.

EXPERIENCING

We Experience the Action of Jesus

A. Discuss the picture on page 19 with your child.

> *Where is Jesus?* (by the tree, in the crowd . . .)
>
> *What is he doing?* (talking, healing, walking, looking at the man . . .)
>
> *Why are so many people around him?* (they want to know him, they are asking for help, they are curious . . .)
>
> *Why is the man sitting in the tree?* (afraid, hiding, wants to see . . .)
>
> *Do you remember a time that you wanted to see and couldn't?*

B. Read the story to your child.

C. Pray the Prayer of Imagination at the end of the story.

D. Responding to the story: Remind your child that the words

> **"Zacchaeus had been changed by Jesus' love"**

come from the story you just read. Because of Jesus' kindness to him, Zacchaeus resolves to reach out to others and to make up for any past wrongs. We, too, may be encouraged to change our lives through the loving example of another.

Give your child time to respond to the two statements in this section. As your child shares the words or pictures he or she has chosen, introduce the theme of forgiveness. When we have sinned, we need to say we are sorry, ask for forgiveness, make amends, and change our hurting ways. Forgiveness is lifelong. The process begins when we help our children recognize the difference between loving and non-loving actions. We help them become aware of how others feel and how their actions affect others. Like Zacchaeus, our children grow as they learn to choose the loving actions of being fair, generous and kind over the non-loving actions of selfishness.

Ask your child:

Can you tell me about a time someone was kind to you?

How did this make you feel? (happy, important, loved . . .)

Did this make you want to be a kind person too?

What are some ways you can be kind to others? (your child may share the answers from page 23 or think of new ones)

What would you like to change in your life? (your child may share the answers from page 23 or go into more detail about one of them)

Sometimes it is hard for us to believe in someone who has resolved to change. Our lack of acceptance makes it more difficult for the person to maintain his or her new way of life. Our children will imitate the way we accept—or don't accept—people who have changed after doing something wrong in the past.

As your child responds to the statements under

"By being loving and forgiving, Jesus helped Zacchaeus to grow"

share the name of a person who helped you to grow. People who love us and believe in us invite us to love and grow. Jesus believed in Zacchaeus even though the crowd did not like him. Jesus showed his belief and love by saying that he wanted to spend the day at Zacchaeus' home.

Ask your child:

Who are the people who love you, who believe in you, who help you grow? (your child may share the answers from page 24 or give new ones)

Who calls you to grow when you have done something wrong? (children usually respond by naming specific people. Mentioning the following categories may help if your child has trouble responding: 1) affirming people who say, "You can do it," "Now let's just try again," "I'll bet you would be good at . . . "; 2) people who help the child choose loving actions; 3) people who help the child take responsibility for having chosen non-loving actions.)

Talk about God's love for each of us, God's belief in our ability to grow as persons. Regardless of what people said about Zacchaeus, Jesus still believed in him. Through his action of forgiving and sharing a meal at the home of Zacchaeus, Jesus reminded the people that God reaches out in love. Zacchaeus changed his life when he realized that Jesus truly loved him. Help your child recall and share experiences in which he or she forgave and was forgiven (page 24).

E. Talk about different ways of showing that we are sorry (a handshake, an apology, an invitation to join in an action or share a meal). Zacchaeus offered to give away half of all he had and if he had cheated anyone, he promised to pay back four times the amount.

Allow time for your child to write a sorry prayer (page 25).

> *Optional:* As a family you may want to write and pray daily your own act of contrition. Family members need to ask for forgiveness and to hear that they are forgiven. How often are these words heard in your family: "I'm sorry," "I was wrong," "Please forgive me," "I forgive you," "Let's try again"? God's forgiveness is often understood through the experience of forgiveness in the family. Our children need to experience the healing, compassion and love that take place in asking for forgiveness, and also in forgiving. We must be an example by asking for forgiveness when we have overreacted, misjudged or treated our children unfairly.
>
> We need to provide our children with an affirming home environment and also effectively teach them to accept responsibility for their actions when things go wrong. We ask:
>
> *What happened?* (Encourage your child to name the action)
>
> *Would you like to talk about it?* (Give your child the chance to admit the wrong)
>
> *What are you going to do about it?* (Give your child the opportunity to make amends)

We Experience the Action of Eucharist

A. Help your child complete the response LORD, HAVE MERCY on page 26.

B. Explain that at the beginning of Mass we confess to God and to one another that we are sorry for our failures to grow in love. Because God loves us, God will always seek us when we are lost. God will always forgive. As the family of God, as people who know we are loved, as the lost ones, we repent our selfishness. In love we reach out to offer or to ask for forgiveness. In silence we remember the times when we have failed to love.

C. In the name of God, the priest and the community forgive us. We respond by saying, "Lord, have mercy," or by saying the *Confiteor* together. Say the *Confiteor* now with your child.

> **I confess to almighty God,**
> **and to you, my brothers and sisters,**
> **that I have sinned through my own fault**
> **in my thoughts and in my words,**
> **in what I have done,**
> **and in what I have failed to do;**
> **and I ask blessed Mary, ever virgin,**
> **all the angels and saints,**
> **and you, my brothers and sisters,**
> **to pray for me to the Lord our God.**

During the celebration of the Eucharist, point out the PENITENTIAL RITE to your child.

We Experience the Action of Family Living

A. Your child may choose to share his or her sorry prayer (page 25) at a family meal. If not, accept the decision willingly.

B. During the meal, ask your child to tell in his or her own words the story of ZACCHAEUS. Discuss ways we can forgive and be forgiven in the family. Be sure to thank your child for sharing.

C. Place a sign (see next page) for ZACCHAEUS on the *Jesus Tree*.

Zacchaeus *(Forgiving)*

PRAYING AT OUR HOME TABLE OF THE LORD

Light the family candle.

Leader: As Zacchaeus experienced forgiveness,
as we experience forgiveness at Mass,
so we also offer and receive forgiveness in our family.

Lord, your love seeks us when we are lost.
Your love invites us to love others.
Forgive us when we fail to love.
Lord, have mercy.

All: **Lord, have mercy.**

Leader: Forgive us when we are unkind.
Christ, have mercy.

All: **Christ, have mercy.**

Leader: Forgive us and help us say we are sorry.
Lord, have mercy.

All: **Lord, have mercy.**

Invite family members to sit in silence as they recall times they may have hurt someone during this day. Encourage them to offer or ask for forgiveness. Then turn to one another and say:

Forgive me if I have hurt you by anything I did or did not do.

Zacchaeus *(Forgiving)*

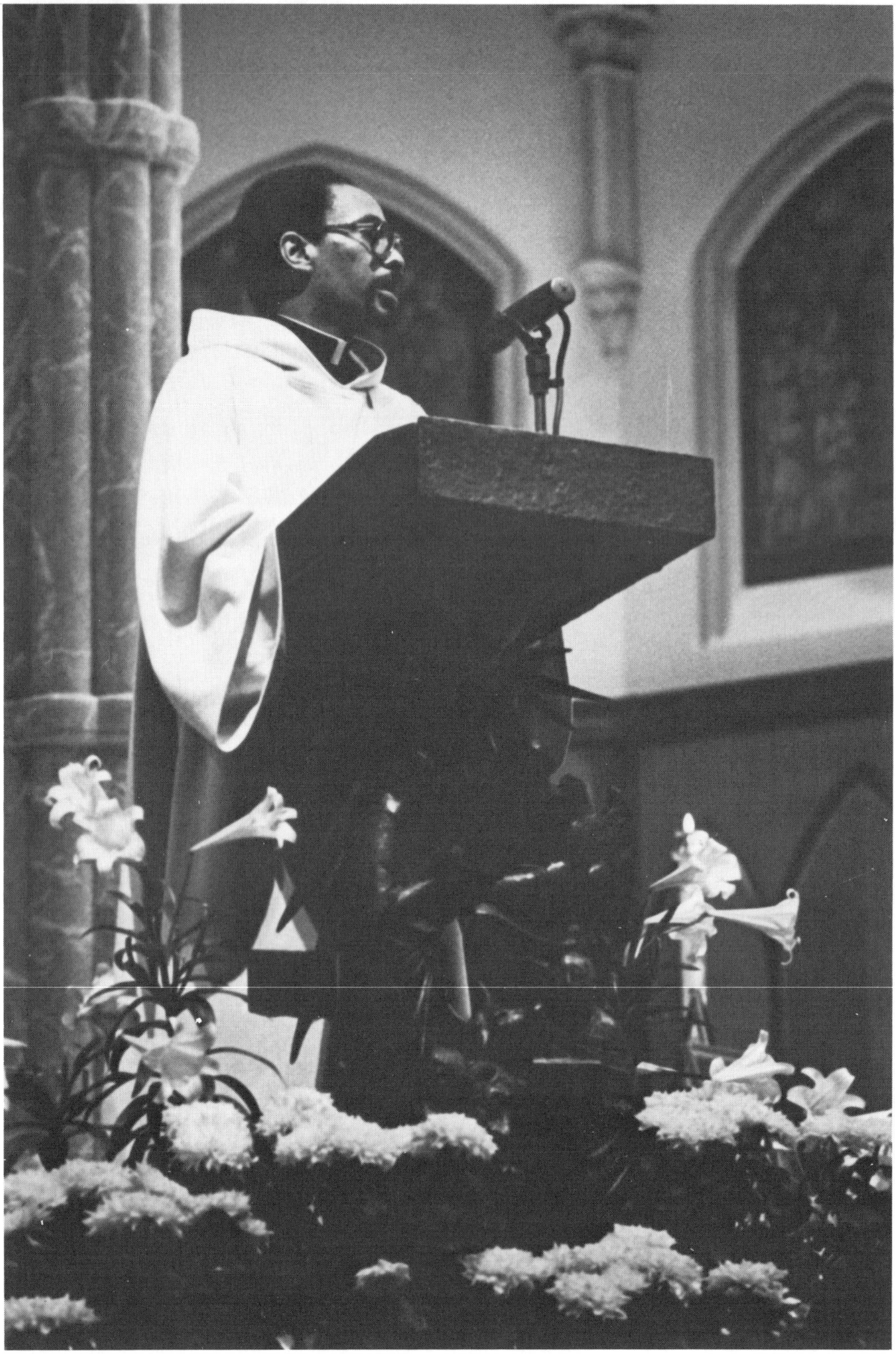

3 Listening

The Good Samaritan

(Luke 10:25-37)

At the Eucharist we listen to the way God speaks to us in scripture, and we respond to God's word.

REFLECTING

We Reflect on the Action of Jesus

Jesus taught the people who came to him, and he teaches us, through his words, deeds and stories. By telling the story of the Good Samaritan, Jesus answered the lawyer's question—Who is my neighbor?—and at the same time showed what it means to be a good neighbor. All people are our neighbors, not only our friends, the people next door, and people who think and act like us, but even those people we don't know, the hurt and lonely, the sick and dying, people we have never met before. We are all God's family, and we must become good neighbors to all our brothers and sisters.

In this story, the Samaritan, the despised foreigner, shows us what it means to be a good neighbor. He was not a learned man. He had not made a study of the law as the lawyer in the story had. But he understood the law of love with his heart. He knew what it meant to be a good neighbor, and in responding compassionately to the needs of another, he lived out God's law.

In living the life of the Eucharist, we too become good neighbors and help people who are in need. We not only hear the words of Jesus, but we live those words.

We Reflect on the Action of Eucharist

During the Liturgy of the Word we listen to readings from scripture. God speaks to us through these words, and it is Jesus, present in his word, who proclaims the gospel. As we stand and sing the Alleluia, we prepare to hear the gospel by praising Christ who comes to us in this good news.

We Reflect on the Action of Family Living

In our families we may find people—mothers, fathers, sisters, brothers, relatives—who are like the Good Samaritan. By listening to their stories and imitating their behavior, we too learn how to be good neighbors. Jesus speaks to us not only in scripture but also through the people who love and care for us. We listen with respect, we pay attention to what family members say, we try to understand not only with our minds but with our hearts. By listening we can discover how to grow. And by listening during the celebration of the Eucharist we can discover Jesus living and present in his word, in the reading of scripture.

EXPERIENCING

We Experience the Action of Jesus

A. Discuss the picture on page 27 with your child.

> *Who are these people?* (mothers, fathers, children, people who need help . . .)
>
> *What are they doing?* (listening to Jesus)
>
> *How can you tell that the people are really listening?* (looking at Jesus, attentive . . .)
>
> *What could Jesus be telling them?* (about God's love for them, to be kind, a story . . .)
>
> *Do you like stories?*
>
> *Do you remember a time when you listened to a story?*
>
> *Who were you listening to?*
>
> *What is your favorite story?*
>
> *Do you remember any stories about Jesus?* (review the stories that you've already told your child: The Wedding at Cana and Zacchaeus)

B. Read the story to your child.

C. Pray the Prayer of Imagination at the end of the story.

D. Responding to the story: Remind your child that the words

"Listen to what he said"

come from the story you just read. Give your child time to respond to the two statements in this section. As you work with your child, introduce the theme of listening. Point out that listening is something we do, not just something that happens to us. It takes effort to listen well. Ask your child to talk about his or her favorite stories. Stories help us remember or understand important things. Jesus told stories because he wanted us to know about God, about ourselves, and about others.

Ask your child:

> *What should you do when you listen to a story?* (pay attention, be respectful, listen with your heart, look at the person . . .)

Emphasize that with so many distractions and sounds in our world, it is hard to be a good listener, but it is an important skill to learn. When we listen and respond to people, their words can help us grow.

> *How do the words of Jesus in this story help us grow?*
>
> *Do you like to tell your family and friends interesting things that happened at school or while you were playing?*
>
> *Do you like them to tell you about people they met and things that were said and done?*

Emphasize that most of us want others to listen to us, but it is also important for us to listen to others. Jesus always wants us to listen to his words. By listening and responding to Jesus' words we can grow to be loving and caring people.

As your child responds to the statements on page 32 under

"Who is my neighbor?"

be sure to mention those neighbors your child might not think of—the poor, the handicapped, people of another race, religion or nationality—so that he or she can begin to understand that all people are our neighbors in the family of God. Ask your child the same question Jesus asked after he told the story of the good Samaritan:

> *"Which one of these acted like a neighbor toward the man attacked by robbers?"*

Then ask:

> *What did he do that showed he was a neighbor?* (he was kind,

The Good Samaritan *(Listening)*

helped the man, bandaged his wounds, took him to the inn, paid for someone to take care of him . . .)

How can you be a good neighbor? (be friendly, help someone, respect the property of others, try to understand how someone feels . . .)

You may want to ask your child to think about these situations:

- A young boy falls off his bicycle and scrapes his knee. What would you do?
- A young girl eats her lunch alone every day at school. She is alone again today. What would you do?

E. Talk about times people in your family have been "good samaritans." Note that by listening to their stories we can learn how to be good neighbors. Jesus speaks to us through these people. All we have to do is listen. Allow time for your child to make the picture on page 33.

We Experience the Action of Eucharist

A. Read the responses we say before and after the reading of the gospel, page 34. Help your child complete the response GLORY TO YOU, LORD.

B. Explain to your child that the Bible (you may want to show your child a bible here) is the most important book ever written. The Bible tells us about God's love for us and the way that love is shown by what God did for the people; it also tells us about Jesus, what he said and did for us, and how the people responded to him. (The three readings from the Bible and the chants between these readings form the main part of the Liturgy of the Word at Mass. Now, however, we will only consider the responses before and after the gospel.)

As a sign of respect we stand as we listen to the gospel reading. When we say the Alleluia, we praise Christ who comes to proclaim the good news. We make small signs of the cross on our forehead, mouth and heart to show our readiness to welcome God's word into our life.

C. When we listen to the word of God, we must also respond to that word. We are hearers and doers. During the homily the priest or deacon helps us discover how to live God's word just as Jesus helped the lawyer see that loving God means helping our neighbor. Before we can live the Eucharist in our daily lives, we have to first listen to what God tells us.

During the celebration of the Eucharist, point out to your child the GOSPEL part of the Mass.

We Experience the Action of Family Living

A. Have your child share his or her picture from page 33 at a family meal.

B. During the meal, ask your child to tell in his or her own words the story of THE GOOD SAMARITAN. Discuss ways we can become good listeners, and ways we can put into action what we hear. Be sure to thank your child for sharing.

C. Place a sign for THE GOOD SAMARITAN on the *Jesus Tree*.

The Good Samaritan *(Listening)*

PRAYING AT OUR HOME TABLE OF THE LORD

Place the bible and the family candle on the dinner table. After the meal, light the candle and pray the following.

Leader: Lord,
We are your family.
Together we listen to your word with our hearts and help one another to live your word.

May we know the word of God.
Make a cross on the forehead.

May we speak the word of God.
Make a cross on the lips.

May we love the word of God.
Make a cross on the heart.

This is a reading from Luke, chapter 10, verse 27.

All: **Glory to you, Lord.**

The leader holds the bible on high for a moment, then lowers it and reads the verse.

Leader: This is the word of the Lord.
Hold the bible on high at the end of the reading.

All: **Praise to you, Lord Jesus Christ.**

Leader: We are happy to live God's word of peace and love with all our neighbors.

All: **Amen.**

4 Caring

The Daughter of Jairus

(Mark 5:21-43)

When we care for and help people in need, we live the Spirit of Jesus in our lives.

REFLECTING

We Reflect on the Action of Jesus

With complete faith in the healing power of Jesus, Jairus asks Jesus to cure his daughter. Jesus always responds to those who believe and even marvels at their faith.

Here is a story of healing, a story of asking and receiving, a miracle story. Like Jairus, we come to Jesus, fall on our knees and say that someone we love needs help. That someone could be in our family, our community, our world; it could be a person we know or someone we have only heard about. As Jesus walked with this distressed father, so he walks with us in all our needs. And as he asked the mother and father of the healed child to care for her, so he asks us to be caretakers for others. By this action, Jesus showed Peter, James and John that they were also to help people in need.

Like Jairus, we need the comforting Spirit of Jesus. Through and with the Spirit of Jesus, the Holy Spirit, we can be sensitive and alert to people in need, show loving compassion, ask Jesus to help them, and care for them in whatever ways we can.

We Reflect on the Action of Eucharist

We come together as brothers and sisters and pray in faith for the needs of all members of the family of God. In prayer we ask God for help not only for those gathered for the Eucharist, but for all people—for the church, for civil authorities, for those with various needs. Every time we celebrate the Eucharist we exercise our priestly function as the family of God by interceding for all people in the General Intercessions (Prayer of the Faithful).

We Reflect on the Action of Family Living

By helping our children take note of the needs of others, we help them develop empathy. Loving compassion for others is a basic step in conscience formation. By our example of caring about and helping those in need, our children learn to express their compassion and care for those who are sick, hurt, sad, lonely, finding difficulty in doing school work, and so on.

Like Jairus, we ask Jesus for help. We invite the Spirit of Jesus to answer our needs and to help us care for the needs of others. We can be Jesus to others; they can be Jesus to us. The presence of the Spirit of Jesus, the Holy Spirit, is alive and active in our families through all the family members—in our immediate families, in the church family, and in the family of all human beings.

EXPERIENCING

We Experience the Action of Jesus

A. Discuss the picture on page 35 with your child.

Who are these people? (mothers, fathers, children, grandparents, friends . . .)

Where is Jesus?

Why are so many people around Jesus? (to listen to him, to ask him for help . . .)

What could some of their problems be? (sickness, sadness, no work, no money, no friends . . .)

Do you remember a time that you asked someone for help?

Can you think of a time you asked Jesus for help?

B. Read the story to your child.

C. Pray the Prayer of Imagination at the end of the story.

D. Responding to the story: Remind your child that the words
"Do not be afraid, only believe"
come from the story you just read. Jesus spoke these words to Jairus when the messengers told him it was too late for help, that his daughter was already dead. No wonder Jairus was afraid!

It is interesting how often Jesus spoke the words "Do not be afraid" to people who needed his help. Sometimes fear paralyzes us. It may prevent us from asking for the help we need or seeing the solution to our problem. Calming the fears of others, as Jesus did with Jairus, is often the first step in helping.

Children at this age have many fears. Invite your child to recall a time he or she was frightened. Then help your child respond to the first statement on page 39.

Jesus asks us to believe, to have faith. It is as a community of believers that we pray. Help your child respond to the second statement on page 39.

After Jesus healed the little girl, he told her parents to take care of her, to give her something to eat. Give your child time to respond to the two statements under the heading on page 40,
"He told them to take care of her."
As your child shares the words or pictures he or she has chosen, talk about caring.

Ask your child:

Who are the people you need in your life? (parents, relatives, friends, doctors, teachers . . .)

Who helps you when you hurt yourself?

Who takes care of you when you are sick?

Help your child become aware of those who care for him or her.

Just as Jesus cared for and helped people in the communities where he lived and traveled, so Jesus is present today in the love and concern people show one another. Jesus traveled to the home of Jairus. Are we willing to go out of our way to show others that we care? And even as Jesus was on the way to the home of Jairus, he remained sensitive to the needs of others. He was aware of the sick woman in the crowd, and he healed her. Do we remain sensitive to the needs of others while we have our minds set on doing something?

How can you show you care about other people? (listening, visiting, helping someone who has a hard time with schoolwork, helping around the house . . .)

The Daughter of Jairus *(Caring)*

We help develop our children's consciences when we foster in them a loving compassion and concern for people in need, when we help them become aware of the needs of others.

E. In prayer we can ask God to make us sensitive to people who need our care, and we can ask God to help them. Recall with your child how comforting it is to have someone take care of you when you are hurt or sick or sad. Jairus asked Jesus, "Please come and place your hands on her, so that she will get well and live." Allow time for your child to list on page 41 those people he or she especially wants to pray for.

> ***Optional:*** At this time you may want to mention to your child the sacrament of the anointing of the sick. In this sacrament we, as a community of believers, ask for God's healing and we show our care and concern for the sick. If your parish anoints the sick regularly at a church service, you might attend with your child. If your child is seriously ill or is to have an operation, you may want to have this special anointing for him or her.

We Experience the Action of Eucharist

A. Help your child complete the words LORD, HEAR OUR PRAYER on page 42.

B. In the communities where he lived, Jesus showed his care for people in need. He asks us to do the same. To help children be aware of these needs, some families post a "We pray for . . . " list in the kitchen. Family members are invited to write the names or initials of those whose needs they want the family to pray for during meal prayers.

C. As a parish family we compose intercessions which are universal, local and current to the changing world. These General Intercessions (Prayer of the Faithful) follow the Profession of Faith. They often include an invitation to pray for individual or family needs.

During the celebration of the Eucharist, point out to your child the time of the GENERAL INTERCESSIONS.

We Experience the Action of Family Living

A. Have your child share the prayer for help (page 41) at a family meal. Encourage your child to talk about what he or she would like Jesus to do for these people. Invite family members to mention other people they would like the family to pray for.

B. During the meal ask your child to tell in his or her own words the story of THE DAUGHTER OF JAIRUS. Discuss ways we can care for others. Be sure to thank your child for sharing.

C. Place a sign for THE DAUGHTER OF JAIRUS on the *Jesus Tree*.

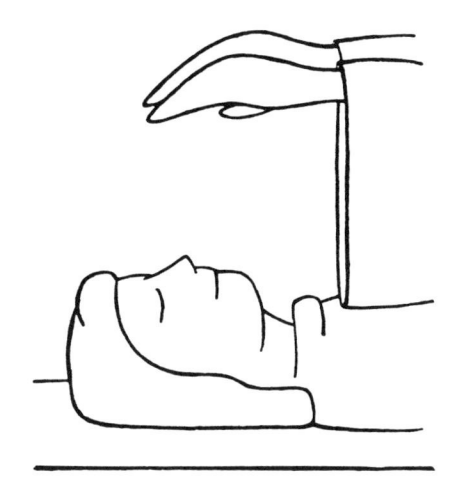

PRAYING AT OUR HOME TABLE OF THE LORD

Place the family blessing cup (filled with wine or juice) on the table.

Leader:	Lord, you call us to care for one another. You want us to show compassion for the sick, the lonely, the unwanted, the unloved. Like Jairus, in faith, we ask for your healing.
	Our response will be, "Lord, hear our prayer."
A Family Member:	We pray for all people who are hurting.

The Daughter of Jairus *(Caring)*

All:	**Lord, hear our prayer.**
A Family Member:	Bring them your healing peace.
All:	**Lord, hear our prayer.**
A Family Member:	Watch over them and keep them in your love.
All:	**Lord, hear our prayer.**
A Family Member:	We pray particularly for *(family members name those they want to pray for)*.
All:	**Lord, hear our prayer.**
Leader:	We pass our blessing cup and say thank you for God's loving care of each of us. As each person drinks from the cup, we pray for the needs of that person.
	Pass the blessing cup.
Leader:	Thank you, Lord, for calling us, your brothers and sisters, to help others. May we know the presence of your Spirit in those people who offer care and help to others.
All:	**Amen.**

THE TABLE OF THE LORD

5 Giving

Martha and Mary

(Luke 10:38-42)

In giving to others, we prepare for the Eucharist where we offer the gifts of bread and wine—and ourselves.

REFLECTING

We Reflect on the Action of Jesus

In this domestic scene Jesus gives us a lesson about two forms of discipleship: active and contemplative. Jesus does not chastise Martha for being a doer, but rather for becoming so anxious and upset about preparing for her guests that she forgets to enjoy them. She is too busy to listen to the words of Jesus.

It seems likely that Jesus often visited these two sisters and their brother Lazarus in their home in Bethany. It is in Bethany that Jesus raises Lazarus from the dead; it is here that Jesus is anointed before going up to Jerusalem for the Last Supper.

How does one prepare for Jesus' visit? Martha prepares one way, Mary another. In the family of God, within our own parish, we prepare for the coming of Jesus in the meal of the Eucharist. We bring the gifts of bread and wine to the altar, thank God for these gifts of creation, and offer ourselves as gift, as one family, to God.

We Reflect on the Action of Eucharist

Many grains of wheat come together to make bread, and many grapes are crushed to make wine. Bread and wine are signs of oneness. In the Eucharist we express our unity as the family of God. During the preparation of the altar and the gifts at the celebration of the Mass, we bring bread and wine to the altar and offer ourselves as gifts to God.

We Reflect on the Action of Family Living

Most of us have both Marthas and Marys in our homes. Through these contrasting temperaments, we learn to respect and appreciate the different ways that people use their talents and gifts in the service of others. There is a time to give through action and a time to serve through prayer. By affirming the gifts of others, we begin to recognize and develop both the Martha and the Mary in each of us.

EXPERIENCING

We Experience the Action of Jesus

A. Discuss the picture on page 43 with your child.

> *Where is Jesus and what is he doing?* (sitting, telling a story, talking about something that has happened . . .)
>
> *What are the two women doing?* (serving food, listening, setting the table . . .)
>
> *Can you remember a time you did one of these things?*

B. Read the story to your child.

C. Pray the Prayer of Imagination at the end of the story.

D. Responding to the story: Remind your child that the words

> **"Mary had the gift of listening. She offered this gift to Jesus,"**

come from the story you just read. When Jesus came to visit, Mary sat at his feet and listened intently to every word he spoke. As your child shares the words or pictures he or she has chosen for page 47, introduce the theme of giving. Point out that we receive gifts at Christmas, on birthdays, and for other special occasions.

Ask your child:

> *What is one gift you received from someone?*
>
> *Who gave you this gift?*
>
> *For what occasion?*

Everything we have is a gift from God—life, parents, trees, animals, earth, sun, the ability to think, feel, laugh and love. Even Jesus is a gift from God.

What are some of your favorite gifts from God?

How do you thank God for these gifts? (go to church, say my prayers, say thank you, use them carefully, share them . . .)

Besides receiving gifts, we also give gifts.

Can you remember a gift you gave to someone?

What is the best gift you could give your parents?

Besides gifts that we buy or make, we can also give a gift by doing something for a person.

What are some things you could do for the members of your family? (love them, help them, listen to them, be nice to them . . .)

Think about Mary's special gift of listening. Giving something of ourselves is the best gift of all.

What are some ways you can give yourself to others? (spend time with them, work with them, make something with them, have fun together . . .)

God has given each person special qualities as gifts. Tell your child how much you appreciate one of his or her gifts (cheerfulness, gentleness, kindness, helpfulness, enthusiasm, thoughtfulness, generosity . . .)

Also think about Martha's gift of action—planning, cooking and serving a meal. Tell your child that you are thankful for his or her "action gifts" too (trying hard in school, playing a musical instrument, participating in sports, doing family chores . . .)

When we share ourselves with others, we ourselves become gifts.

Ask:

What persons do you love so much that you would like to wrap them as gifts to share with others?

One of God's very special gifts to us is the gift of one another. Our proper response to God is thank you.

Have your child respond to the statements on page 48 under the headings

"You are worried and troubled over so many things"

and

"She sat down at his feet and listened."

Martha and Mary *(Giving)*

When we can share our worries with others, we take the first step in dealing constructively with them. There is an honesty about Martha as she voices her frustration.

Ask your child:

When do you worry most? (at night, when I have no friends, when I have too many things to do, at school . . .)

Who listens to your worries? (parents, teacher, friends, brothers or sisters . . .)

When we have many things to do, we sometimes become fretful and forget our reasons for doing them to begin with. In this incident at the home of Martha and Mary, we see that it is not the amount of food or the preparation that makes the meal special, but rather hearing the words of Jesus. Jesus often speaks to us today in the words of those around us. We have to keep our preparations simple enough so that we can hear the people present. It is not how much we do, but how much love we put in the doing that matters most. Mary takes the time to enjoy the friendship of Jesus. Nothing else is that important.

Sometimes we are like Martha, sometimes like Mary. Jesus wants us to be both hearers (Mary) and doers (Martha) of his word.

Ask:

In what way could you be a hearer? (listen to the readings in church, read the Bible, listen to parents and teachers . . .)

In what way could you be a doer? (help with younger children, do an extra job at home, save some money or collect canned goods for the poor, save clothes for the St. Vincent de Paul Society . . .)

E. Talk about the preparations needed for a meal. Planning a menu, shopping for food, cooking, setting the table, and blessing the food are wonderful gifts to give others. You may want to have a family night with each family member selecting a way to contribute to the meal preparations. Then offer this meal to one another as a gift. And, by listening and sharing during the meal, give of yourselves as well. Allow time for your child to plan a menu and make a picture of the family table set with favorite foods (page 49).

> ### Family Tablecloth
>
> Make a tablecloth for your home table of the Lord. Place a sheet on the table. Outline an area the size of a placemat for each family member. Then invite each person to draw in this "mat" his or her favorite gifts of creation. Suggest that each family member add his or her name as a sign of willingness to become a gift for others. In the center of the tablecloth draw wheat and bread, grapes and wine. Explain that long ago people offered the first fruits of the harvest to God. They asked God to bless their offering. At our home table of the Lord and at our church table of the Lord, we prepare, bring and offer gifts as family.

We Experience the Action of the Eucharist

A. Help your child complete the words BLESSED BE GOD FOREVER, the response we give when the priest offers bread and wine in our name (page 50).

B. We prepare the altar table for a special meal by placing bread and wine on it. Explain that these gifts are brought to the altar by members of the family of God. These simple gifts show our gratitude for the goods of the earth which we all have and use. The money collected for the church and the poor is presented also. In song or in silence we prepare in our hearts for Jesus as we set the table of the Lord.

We also offer ourselves. We bring all the actions of our daily living to the altar. Our gifts are received and God is thanked. We prepare ourselves to receive God's greatest gift to us—Jesus.

C. During the celebration of the Eucharist, point out to your child the time of THE PREPARATION OF THE ALTAR AND THE GIFTS.

We Experience the Action of Family Living

A. Have your child share the menu and picture on page 49 at a family meal. Use your specially made tablecloth at this meal. Ask family members to share their drawings of God's gifts. Thank God together for these gifts.

Martha and Mary *(Giving)*

B. During the meal, ask your child to tell in his or her own words the story of MARTHA AND MARY. Discuss ways we can give ourselves to one another. Be sure to thank your child for sharing.

C. Place a sign for MARTHA AND MARY on the *Jesus Tree*.

PRAYING AT OUR HOME TABLE OF THE LORD

Use your tablecloth for your home table of the Lord for this meal. Place the family blessing cup (filled with wine or juice) on the table.

Leader:	Lord, As the gifts at the Eucharist are blessed by the priest, so we bless the gifts at our home meals. Our tablecloth reminds us of the many gifts which are ours. Our response will be, "Blessed be God forever."
Leader:	For the gift of the good earth,
All:	**Blessed be God forever.**
Leader:	For the gift of the food on our table,
All:	**Blessed be God forever.**
Leader:	For the gift of the people who prepared our food,
All:	**Blessed be God forever.**

Leader: For the gift of being together as family,

All: **Blessed be God forever.**

Leader: For the gift of the Marthas and Marys in our lives,

All: **Blessed be God forever.**

Leader: For the gift of the Lord in our daily living,

All: **Blessed be God forever.**

Leader: In silence we pass our blessing cup and thank God for the many blessings of this day.

Pass the cup.

Leader: Let us join hands as we say the family blessing.

All: **Bless us, O Lord,
and these your gifts,
which we are about to receive from your bounty,
through Christ our Lord. Amen.**

Martha and Mary *(Giving)*

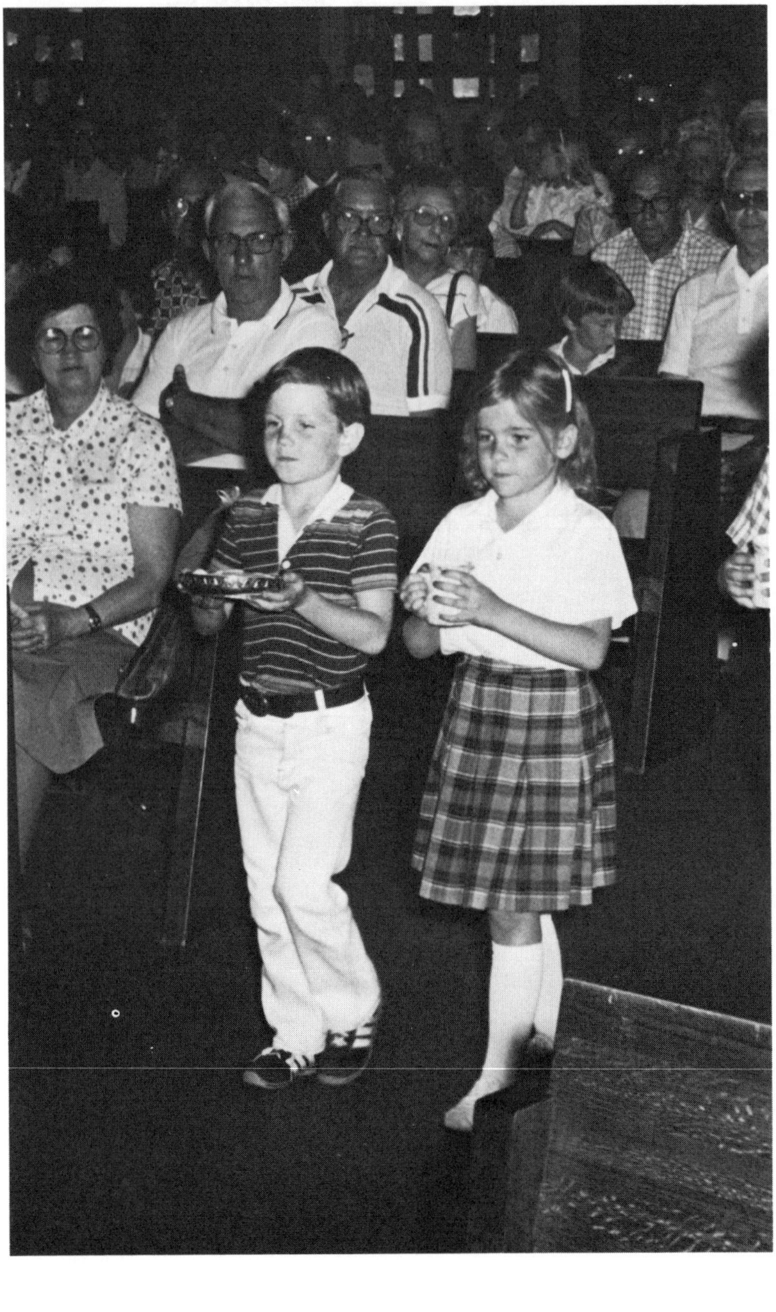

6 Sharing

Jesus Feeds the 5,000

(John 6:1-11)

When we share, we live the life of the Eucharist.

REFLECTING

We Reflect on the Action of Jesus

Jesus gives himself to us when we share with one another. A poignant example of sharing is offered in the story of the feeding of the 5,000: A boy willingly gives the little bit of food that he has with him, even though it seems pointless in terms of the size of the crowd. Jesus gives thanks to God, and in his hands the boy's insignificant gift becomes all that is needed, and more.

In this story we notice that Jesus asked the apostles to give the people something to eat, to provide for them. Jesus himself had been healing them, speaking of God's love for them, and offering them words of comfort and care. Now he asks the apostles to imitate his sharing actions by feeding them.

The next day Jesus will explain to this same crowd that he is the bread of life: "He who comes to me will never be hungry; he who believes in me will never be thirsty" (Jn 6:35). The ordinary bread satisfied the physical hunger of the 5,000. But now Jesus invites the people to more, to share in his very life: "I am the living bread that came down from heaven. If anyone eats this bread he will live forever" (Jn 6:51). Whenever we come to the meal of the Eucharist, we share the life of Jesus through the bread of life and through the people gathered.

We Reflect on the Action of Eucharist

During the celebration of the Mass, the gifts of bread and wine are prepared, and the celebrant prays over them asking God that they become our nourishment, the bread of life. During the dialogue which opens the Eucharistic Prayer, we join with the celebrant in giving thanks for the love God shares with us as family. In this dialogue we are reminded of our close union with the priest and with one another as we thank the Father through Jesus.

We Reflect on the Action of Family Living

Every day brings us many opportunities to show our love by responding to the needs of others, and by thanking others for their care and help. Members of our families correct us when we do wrong, praise us when we do a good job, listen to us when we share the news of our day, care about us. It is through them, and others outside our families, that Jesus gives us what we need.

When we eat a family meal, we give thanks for the gifts that others have shared with us. In the meal of the Eucharist, we give thanks to God for sharing Jesus with us.

EXPERIENCING

We Experience the Action of Jesus

A. Discuss the picture on page 51 with your child.

Who are these people? (Jesus, some children, a crowd . . .)

What are they doing? (listening, having a picnic, talking . . .)

What is Jesus doing? (blessing the food, sitting, taking care of the people . . .)

Encourage your child to share with you the different people and actions in this picture—giving, receiving, sharing, listening, caring, and so forth.

B. Read the story to your child

C. Pray the Prayer of Imagination at the end of the story.

D. Responding to the story: Remind your child that the words

**"There is a boy here who has five loaves of
barley bread and two fish"**

come from the story you just read. Give your child time to respond to the two statements in this section. As your child shares the words or pictures he or she has chosen, introduce the theme of sharing. As parents, it is interesting to consider the home environment of this boy who was so willing to share all that he had (the five loaves of barley bread and the two fish) with others who were strangers to him. Certainly he must have been following the example of family members in being so generous. Even so, it must have been difficult for him to share all he had without the promise of something in return. Our children—and ourselves perhaps—want to insure that they will receive something in return for what they do. It is not easy for young children to share graciously. We need to encourage their growth in sharing, yet at the same time respect and understand their feelings of insecurity and reluctance in sharing what they have and who they are with others.

Ask your child:

Is it hard to share certain games or toys when playing with friends? If so, which ones?

When taking turns would you choose to go first, be in the middle, or go last? How do you feel when you go first? When you go last?

Besides sharing things, how else can you share with others? (a smile, a kind word, spending time with someone . . .)

Can you think of a time when you were like this boy, when you shared what you had? How did you feel when you did this? (proud, happy, like Jesus, scared then glad . . .)

Is it hard to say thank you when someone shares with you? How do you feel when someone thanks you for what you have shared? (easier to say thank you, I feel funny when someone says thank you, it feels good to have someone thank me, I forget sometimes . . .)

In this story we learn that Jesus wants us to share and to show our appreciation when others share with us. Tell your child how much you enjoy sharing this preparation for first Eucharist with him or her. Show your appreciation by saying thank you for the way your child shares the pictures and words chosen in response to the story.

As your child responds to the statements on page 56 under

**"Jesus gave the bread and fish to the apostles
to share with the people"**

explain to your child that Jesus usually gives us what we need through other people. The Spirit of Jesus in us helps us to share with

Jesus Feeds the 5,000 *(Sharing)*

one another, to help people in need, and to receive from others. In the beginning of the story, Jesus shared his love with the people by healing, listening and talking with them. Jesus could have also provided food for them directly, but instead he let the young boy be an example of his message in action. Further, he wanted the apostles—and he wants us—to imitate him by taking care of his people. Tell your child incidents or the names of people in your life who have shared their love and care with you. Point out that Jesus wants us to share food with those who are hungry, but he also means for us to be aware of people's other needs and to help whenever we are able.

Ask your child:

How do you feel when you are hungry and someone gives you something to eat right then? (good, happy, lucky . . .)

Who usually gives you food when you are hungry? (parents, grandparents, relatives, friends, a neighbor . . .)

Have you ever been to a large picnic? If so, how does it feel to eat outdoors with a large group of people? (fun, friendly, a little scary . . .)

Who are some of the people in our world who are hungry? (the poor, children in poor countries, people without jobs . . .)

Who shares food with them? (the government, churches, other people . . .)

> ***Note:*** Most American children think of hunger as a problem only in far-away places. Taking part in food drives at Thanksgiving or Christmas (or on Food Sunday each month if your parish has this activity) and gathering clothing and toys for the Saint Vincent de Paul Society or other charitable organizations can help your child become aware that there are people in need quite close to home. We want to become sensitive to the needs of brothers and sisters both far away and close to home.

When we share with others, we are doing what Jesus asked of us. And when we thank others, we are thanking Jesus. Encourage your child to thank Jesus often for his Spirit which helps us to share with one another.

E. Talk about ways we can thank others for helping us, for sharing their time and lives with us. Note that Jesus gave thanks to his Father. Help your child write a prayer of thanks or find an appropriate picture for page 57.

We Experience the Action of Eucharist

A. Help your child complete the words IT IS RIGHT TO GIVE HIM THANKS AND PRAISE from the dialogue which open the Eucharistic Prayer, on page 58.

B. The theme of thanksgiving permeates the whole Eucharistic Prayer of the Mass. This element of thanksgiving is clearly focused in the preface and in the dialogue which leads to the preface. With hands extended, the celebrant invites us through this dialogue to give thanks for all that God has shared with us. Explain that our response is a thanksgiving prayer, a time in the Mass to think of all the gifts God has shared with us—the beauty of creation, the love of people, the presence of Jesus in our lives today through the gift of the Spirit.

C. During the celebration of the Eucharist, point out to your child the gestures of the priest as he invites everyone to join in the dialogue which begins the EUCHARISTIC PRAYER.

We Experience the Action of Family Living

A. Have your child share his or her prayer of thanks (page 57) at a family meal.

B. During the meal, ask your child to tell in his or her own words the story of THE FEEDING OF THE 5,000. Discuss ways your family can be like Jesus and share with others. Be sure to thank your child for sharing.

C. Place a sign (see next page) for THE FEEDING OF THE 5,000 on the *Jesus Tree.*

PRAYING AT OUR HOME TABLE OF THE LORD

Pray the prayer of thanks your child has completed or use the following family meal blessing.

Place the family candle on the table. Also have an unsliced loaf of bread on a cutting board. For the main dish, prepare something that can be sliced and served at the table — roast meat, chicken, fish, meat loaf—or a casserole.

Leader:	Lord, Come and bless our family meal. Lift up your hearts.
All:	**We lift them up to the Lord.**
Leader:	Let us give thanks to the Lord our God.
All:	**It is right to give him thanks and praise.**

The mother lights the candle and says,

Mother:	We light this candle to show that our family wants to share the light and life of Jesus with others.

Litany

Leader: Our response will be: "We give thanks, O Lord."
For the people who grow and prepare the food we eat,

All: **We give thanks, O Lord.**

Leader: For helping us live with a generous heart,

All: **We give thanks, O Lord.**

Leader: For the living bread of life which you share with us in the Eucharist,

All: **We give thanks, O Lord.**

Leader: For the gift of the Spirit who helps us share with one another,

All: **We give thanks, O Lord.**

The leader invites the family members to add their own prayers of thanksgiving. After the last response, ask one family member to slice the bread and pass it out. Another serves the main dish. When the plates are filled, say together,

All: **Bless us, O Lord,
and these your gifts,
which we are about to receive from your
   bounty,
through Christ our Lord. Amen.**

Jesus Feeds the 5,000 *(Sharing)*

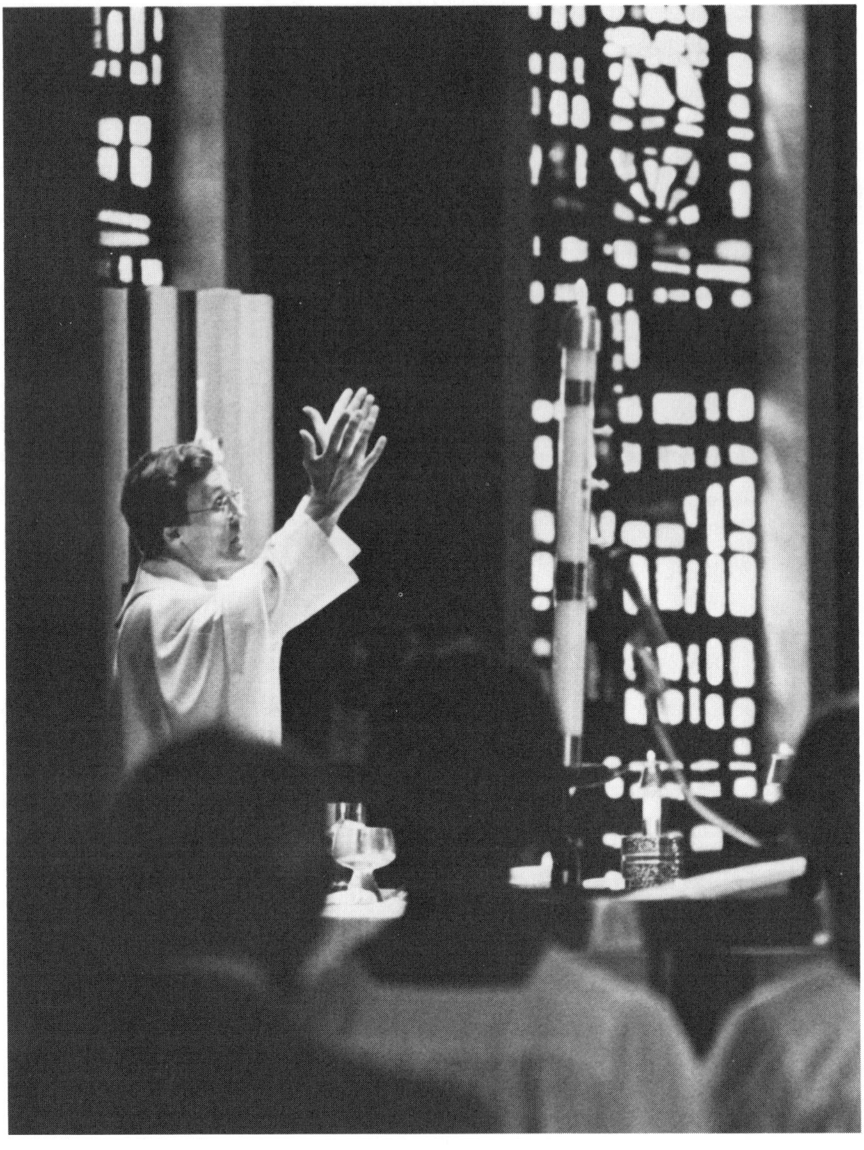

7 Remembering

The Last Supper

(Luke 22:7-20)

In the meal of the Eucharist we remember Jesus' love for us.

REFLECTING

We Reflect on the Action of Jesus

At the Passover meal the Jewish people remember God's great love for them. Jesus and his friends gathered to celebrate this meal, and Jesus used the occasion to offer himself as a sacrifice for us all. In sharing the bread and wine, he said, "This is my body . . . This is my blood." In scripture the term *body* means the whole person, and the term *blood* means a person's whole life. Jesus offered everything he was and asks us to do the same: "Do this in memory of me."

Jesus ate many meals with his friends, but this last meal before his death is a special one. We continue to partake in this same special meal today in the Eucharist as we celebrate and remember his life, his death and resurrection. By sharing this same meal of the Eucharist, we express and affirm our belief that the whole mystery of the risen Christ is present and active in the Mass as we gather, eat and drink as the people of God. Nourished by this meal, we go forth to show our love as Jesus did, to give our lives as he did—for others.

We Reflect on the Action of Eucharist

During the Eucharist we are asked to proclaim the mystery of faith in response to the words of institution (consecration). The words of institution are part of the Eucharistic Prayer which is a thanksgiving prayer of praise. The mystery of faith is the paschal mystery—the mystery of Christ's death, rising, and presence among his people. In the Eucharist we remember the past—the Last Supper and Jesus' sacrifice of his life for us on the cross—and we celebrate his sacrifice here and now in a special way. We give thanks for what Jesus has done; we meet him present among the people gathered; and we look forward to the future when we will eat the meal of the kingdom. While our primary-age children will not wholly understand this eucharistic action, they can understand and believe that Jesus is present in the meal of the Eucharist and that the bread is Christ's Body and the wine is Christ's Blood.

We Reflect on the Action of Family Living

Every day, and sometimes several times a day, we gather around our family table to share food and the experiences of our day. At this table we know the presence of God through each family member. At the Last Supper, at the Eucharist, and at our family meal, friends share at the table of the Lord. At this table we remember the love Jesus has for us and the love we have for him and for one another. Through this love we know we are blessed, and that here at the table of the Lord everything and everyone can be made whole.

EXPERIENCING

We Experience the Action of Jesus

A. Discuss the picture on page 59 with your child.

How many people are sitting at this table? (13)

Who are they? (Jesus and his 12 apostles)

What are they doing? (talking, listening, eating, having fun . . .)

Why are they at this meal? (they were hungry, it's a party, they were invited . . .)

Where is Jesus? (in the center, with his friends . . .)

What is he doing? (breaking the bread, talking with the apostles . . .)

What kind of food is on the table? (bread, wine . . .)

> *Note:* Besides bread and wine, a Passover meal could include hard-cooked eggs, salt or vinegar, herbs, fruit and nuts sprinkled with ginger, and roast lamb.

Do you remember a special meal you ate once with your family?

B. Read the story to your child.

C. Pray the Prayer of Imagination at the end of the story.

D. Responding to the story: Remind your child that the words

**"Jesus wanted his friends to remember him and his love—
to remember all the words he spoke and the
loving and kind things he did"**

come from the story you just read. Introduce the theme of remembering. You might look through the photos in your family album or name some of the special things that have happened in your family. Ask your child to choose one time and write or draw the event to complete the first statement on page 63.

Ask your child:

What happened? (the past)

How do you feel when you remember this event? (the present)

Do you look forward to doing something like this again? (the future)

It is in the act of remembering that we keep people and events alive and present to us now and take them with us into the future.

To be a member of a faith community is to have a common memory of events that have formed us. In remembering the actions of the Last Supper through the celebration of the Eucharist we partake in a common memory of an event that has shaped and continues to shape our life today as a faith community. Help your child remember things that Jesus did—his love for others, the words he spoke, the suffering he offered for us, his teachings. Looking at the symbols on your *Jesus Tree* will help recall the stories about Jesus you have read together. Choose one of these times and respond to the second statement on page 63.

The Last Supper *(Remembering)*

To help your child respond to the first statement on page 64 under the heading

"Do this in memory of me"

talk about the actions of Jesus and the people at the Last Supper. You may want to pantomime these actions of Jesus.

Ask your child:

> *What did Jesus do with the bread?* (took, gave thanks, broke, gave to friends)
>
> *What did Jesus do with the wine?* (took, gave thanks, gave to friends)
>
> *What words show that Jesus gave himself?* (This is my body which is given for you.)
>
> *Who did Jesus invite to the Last Supper?* (friends)
>
> *What did they do?* (ate the meal, felt one with Jesus, talked, enjoyed one another . . .)
>
> *What did Jesus ask them to do in the future?* (celebrate this meal always in memory of him)

Celebrations help to bring a memory into the present and to anticipate a future. Jesus used a meal so that we could remember his love for us, a love so great that he gave his life to us. However, the eucharistic prayer is not just nostalgic dreaming or remembering. It is the response we make as God's people to Jesus' command in the scripture to "Do this in memory of me." Christ, our faith tells us, is actually present among us in the breaking of the bread. The meal we eat is the gift of Christ himself as food. As we participate in the actions of sharing the meal, in the eating of the bread, in the drinking of the cup, in the gathering of the people, we know Jesus is present as he was present at the Last Supper and will be present in the final gathering of his people.

Respond to the second statement on page 64. While our understanding of the presence of God in the assembly has gained a new emphasis and importance, it is not the same as the presence of Christ in the Eucharist. They are uniquely different and the church has always celebrated the eucharistic presence of Christ as the central mystery of our faith. Remind your child that the bread is Christ's body and the wine is Christ's blood. As your child considers actions he or she can do this week in memory of Jesus, explain that whenever we celebrate the meal of the Eucharist and offer ourselves as a self-gift to

God and God's people, we do as Jesus did when he offered himself as a self-gift for us on the cross, we act in memory of him.

We have emphasized Eucharist as meal throughout this program, but you will also want your child to be aware of the Eucharist as sacrifice. Jesus lived his whole life for others. In a great act of love, he even gave up his life for us on the cross. We remember that Christ sacrificed his life because he loved us and continues to do this every time we celebrate the Eucharist. When the priest says, "This is my body, which is given for you," the words "given for you" remind us that Jesus died, rose, and will come again—all for love of us. Discuss how we can sacrifice for others, show love to others, ways we can give and share our life with others. We do these actions in memory of Jesus.

E. Jesus ate many meals with his friends where he shared bread and wine. Explain to your child that Jesus wanted his followers to remember him in the simple everyday actions of eating and drinking, so he choose common food.

He took food that people of all times and places have used for sustenance—bread and wine—and made them special at the meal of the Last Supper. The bread was and is Christ's body; the wine was and is Christ's blood. While the appearances of bread and wine remain, the reality is the body and blood of Christ.

In the eating of the bread, the drinking of the cup, in the people gathered, Jesus is present in the meal of the Eucharist as he was present in the special meal of the Last Supper. The actions and words of Jesus and apostles at the Last Supper are the same actions and words we celebrate today in the Eucharist. Ordinary bread and wine become special; they become Jesus.

> *Note:* To understand that the Eucharist is something more than ordinary bread and wine, and to want to receive Jesus in the Eucharist, are the minimum requirements for First Communion.

Help your child see the similarities between the Last Supper and the Mass—the presence of Jesus, the people gathered around the table of the Lord, the bread and the wine. Illustrate the meals on page 65.

The Last Supper *(Remembering)*

We Experience the Action of Eucharist

A. Help your child complete the words CHRIST HAS DIED, CHRIST IS RISEN, CHRIST WILL COME AGAIN, on page 66.

B. After the priest pronounces the words of blessing over the bread and wine, he asks us to proclaim through one of the four Memorial Acclamations the mystery of our faith—the paschal mystery of Jesus dying, rising, and being present among his people.

C. During the celebration of the Eucharist, point out to your child the MEMORIAL ACCLAMATION.

We Experience the Action of Family Living

A. Have your child share his or her pictures of the Last Supper and the Eucharist at a family meal.

B. During the meal, ask your child to tell in his or her own words the story of THE LAST SUPPER. Note that Jesus is present today in a special way in the meal of the Eucharist, and that he is also present in another way as we gather for our family meal.

C. Place a sign for THE LAST SUPPER on the *Jesus Tree*.

Optional:

A Home Table of the Lord Prayer

At Mass we bring not only bread and wine to the parish table of the Lord, but also the experiences we have had during the week and Jesus' presence in those experiences. With your family recall and write down some of your experiences around your family table during the past year. Recognize that Jesus is present in the people gathered in your home.

For Example:

"Around this table 300 graces have been said, dreams have been shared, and homework done. Card games have been played here, and birthdays and anniversaries have been celebrated. . . ."

Add successes, failures, times of forgiveness, people and things you enjoyed doing . . . anything and everything you have shared as a family among yourselves and with others.

"And when we share the cup, we share in the stories of each person present. We share one another's burdens, heartaches and joys. And we know we are blessed, for at the table of the Lord everything and everyone is made whole."

Say this prayer at special family meals. Use it often as your family prayer of remembrance.

PRAYING AT OUR HOME TABLE OF THE LORD

Place your family table of the Lord cloth and the family blessing cup (filled with wine or juice) on the table.

Leader: Lord,
We thank you for your table at the Last Supper where you shared a special meal with your friends.

The Last Supper *(Remembering)*

Because of your presence, Lord, our home table is
  holy,
and so are we who come to share this meal.
Lord,
You love us.
Help us to remember your love.
Help us to remember that you are with us in
  everything we do.
Whenever we share a meal, let us know of your
  presence.
Let us remember the way you gave your life for us.
As we silently pass our blessing cup and drink from
  it,
we remember your love for us and thank you for
  your blessings.

Pass the blessing cup.

Leader: We offer love to one another,
your love in us.

Turn to each person present and say,

_____*(Name)*_____, remember that God loves you. Remember that I love you, too.

Sing one of the four memorial acclamations from the Mass or read your home table of the Lord prayer.

8 Belonging

The Breakfast at the Lake

(John 21:1-14)

In the Eucharist we are one with Jesus and one with each other. We belong.

REFLECTING

We Reflect on the Action of Jesus

In this third appearance after his resurrection, Jesus came to his apostles at the side of a lake. He prepared breakfast and ate with them. To this meal the apostles brought their frustration of working together all night and catching no fish as well as their pleasure in suddenly making a huge catch. Meals with our friends and family deepen our understanding of one another. Like the apostles, we too bring our experiences to our family meals, and to the meal of the Eucharist.

In this breakfast meal among close friends—Jesus and his apostles—we see a sign of the Eucharist. In thanksgiving that we are loved and that we belong to God as family, we say yes to the invitation of Jesus to "come and eat." Like the apostles, we bring our life experiences to one another and to the Lord, and we rejoice that we are together again.

We Reflect on the Action of Eucharist

At Mass we respond to Jesus' invitation to gather in joy. Before we receive the meal of the Eucharist, we show our oneness with Jesus and with all our brothers and sisters in the church. Together we say the Our Father, a special prayer which emphasizes that we are the family of God, and we offer a sign of peace to one another.

We Reflect on the Action of Family Living

We can provide opportunities in our home for all family members to feel loved and enjoy a sense of belonging. We can work, play and pray together. We can offer signs of peace—a hug, a smile, a kiss, a wink, a word—that show we are willing to be one even with all our differences.

In the Mass we receive Jesus in the eucharistic meal, and we also receive him through our brothers and sisters gathered for the celebration. When we eat a family meal, we receive the food, but we also receive one another as we share the day's experiences. And we receive Jesus through one another.

EXPERIENCING

We Experience the Action of Jesus

A. Discuss the picture on page 67 with your child.

> *Who could these people be?* (campers, fishermen . . .)
>
> *What are they doing?* (cooking, camping, eating, talking, planning . . .)
>
> *Can you remember a time when you did the same thing?*
>
> *Could one of these men be Jesus?*
>
> *Which one?*
>
> *What is he doing?*
>
> *What are some of the other people in the picture doing?*

B. Read the story to your child.

C. Pray the Prayer of Imagination at the end of the story.

D. Responding to the story: Remind your child that the words

"We will come with you"

come from the story you just read. When Peter decided to go fishing, his friends said, "We will come with you." Give your child time to respond to the two statements on page 71. As your child shares the words or pictures he or she has chosen, introduce the theme of belonging. Talk about what it means to belong to a family, to a group, to Jesus.

Ask your child:

> *What are some of the things you like to do as a family?* (go to the beach, eat out at a restaurant, go to Grandma and Grandpa's, see a movie . . .)
>
> *What are some of the things you like to do with your friends?* (ride bikes, play ball, go for an ice cream cone . . .)
>
> *What are some of the things the friends of Jesus did together?* (went fishing, traveled, shared meals . . .)
>
> *How do you feel when a friend invites you to share a meal— maybe a birthday celebration?*
>
> *How do you think Jesus' friends felt when they were invited to breakfast?* (special, thought of, cared about, one of the group, accepted, happy . . .)

Emphasize that because Jesus is our brother, we are all family, all friends with each other and with him. We belong together.

As your child responds to the statements on page 72 under the heading

"They belonged with one another"

share ways your family (home family, school family, parish family, even world family) has grown during the past week: in forgiving, in working together, in playing, in praying, in listening, in showing love and peace to one another. Explain that Jesus is present not only at the meals we eat, for example, but also in the people who gather at our table. He is present in the special bread of the Mass—the Eucharist—and he is present in the people who gather for this eucharistic meal.

E. Talk about the different members of your family. Include grandparents, aunts, uncles and cousins, especially if your immediate family is small. Recall different meals you have had together. Note that when one person is not present for a family meal, especially a celebration, that person is missed.

Consider how happy the friends of Jesus were to be with him again. They belonged with him, and we belong to him and to one another.

Allow time for your child to draw a picture of your family sharing a meal (page 73).

The Breakfast at the Lake *(Belonging)*

Optional:

On Baptism

Besides belonging to a home family, your child also belongs to the family of God. As we grow in our home family, so we grow in God's family. Baptism is the sacrament that first marks our initiation into membership in the church, the faith community. Through the sacraments of confirmation and Eucharist, we complete the stages of initiation.

Children love to hear about their baptism. Share with your child what happened on that day, the people present at the celebration, the reasons why you chose the godparents you did. Share the reasons you promised to help your child grow in faith. If you have any pictures of this day, be sure to show them to your child.

Talk about your child's name and the importance of a name in telling others who we are. Explain why you chose this name. Help your child remember that we are loved so much that God calls each of us by name. In the name of the faith community, the priest accepted that name and welcomed the child.

You might want to share with your child what you did at the baptism to show your faith and love:

- we asked that you be baptized
- we signed you with the sign of the cross
- we professed our faith
- we carried you to the baptismal font

    (Water was poured on your head and the words of baptism spoken. You were anointed with holy chrism.)

- we received your white garment
- we held the lighted candle
- we said the Our Father
- we were blessed

Help your child fill in the baptism certificate at the back of the *Child's Book*.

Mark the anniversary of your child's baptism on your family calendar and plan a celebration for that special day.

We Experience the Action of Eucharist

A. Help your child complete the words OUR FATHER and the response we give at the Sign of Peace, AND ALSO WITH YOU (page 74).

B. Explain that Jesus himself taught us to pray by giving us the Our Father. Point out that we show we are brothers and sisters by calling God our Father. Say this prayer for your child:

> **Our Father, who art in heaven,**
>   **hallowed be thy Name;**
> **thy kingdom come;**
> **thy will be done on earth**
>   **as it is in heaven.**
> **Give us this day our daily bread;**
> **and forgive us our trespasses**
> **as we forgive those who trespass against us;**
> **and lead us not into temptation,**
> **but deliver us from evil.**

C. At the Sign of Peace at Mass we offer a prayer and a gesture—the words *Peace* or *Peace be with you* and a handshake, a nod, a hug or a kiss. We are expressing our love and friendship for all the people present.

> *What are some ways to offer family members a sign of peace?*
> (a kiss, a favorite treat, a sincere compliment . . .)

Choose one way and offer one another a sign of peace at dinner.

During the celebration of the Eucharist, point out to your child the time to pray the OUR FATHER and to offer the SIGN OF PEACE.

We Experience the Action of Family Living

A. Have your child share the picture of your family at a family meal (page 73). Encourage him or her to talk about the picture—but don't insist.

B. During the meal, ask your child to tell in his or her own words the story of THE BREAKFAST AT THE LAKE. Discuss ways we

The Breakfast at the Lake *(Belonging)*

can continue to grow in oneness with Jesus and with one another. Be sure to thank your child for sharing.

C. Place a sign for THE BREAKFAST AT THE LAKE on the *Jesus Tree*.

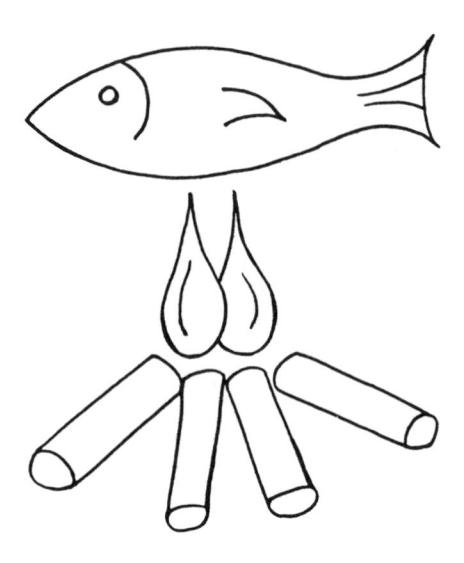

PRAYING AT OUR HOME TABLE OF THE LORD

Place the family candle on the table.

Leader: Lord,
We are your family.
We belong to you and to one another.
As we gather around our home table of the Lord
and light this family candle,
we bless our table and each person present.
In the striking of the match we light a memory,
a memory of all the times family members have
    come together to eat,
    to celebrate,
    to show our oneness.

Our response will be, "Come and eat."

Leader: Lord, we are your precious people. You call us to your table. We thank you for our grandparents, and with you we say . . .

All:	**Come and eat.**
Leader:	We thank you for aunts, uncles, cousins, and with you we say . . .
All:	**Come and eat.**
Leader:	We thank you for friends, and with you we say . . .
All:	**Come and eat.**
Leader:	We thank you for each person present, for _____*(names)*_____, and with you we say . . .
All:	**Come and eat.**
Leader:	We thank you for the people who gather at the Eucharist, and with you we say . . .
All:	**Come and eat.**
Leader:	Let us join hands and pray the Our Father to show we are family.

All:	**Our Father, who art in heaven,**
	    hallowed be thy Name;
	thy kingdom come;
	thy will be done on earth
	    as it is in heaven.
	Give us this day our daily bread;
	and forgive us our trespasses
	as we forgive those who trespass against us;
	and lead us not into temptation,
	but deliver us from evil. Amen.

Leader:	Let us extend a thank you by offering a sign of peace and saying to one another, "Thank you for being in my family."

The Breakfast at the Lake *(Belonging)*

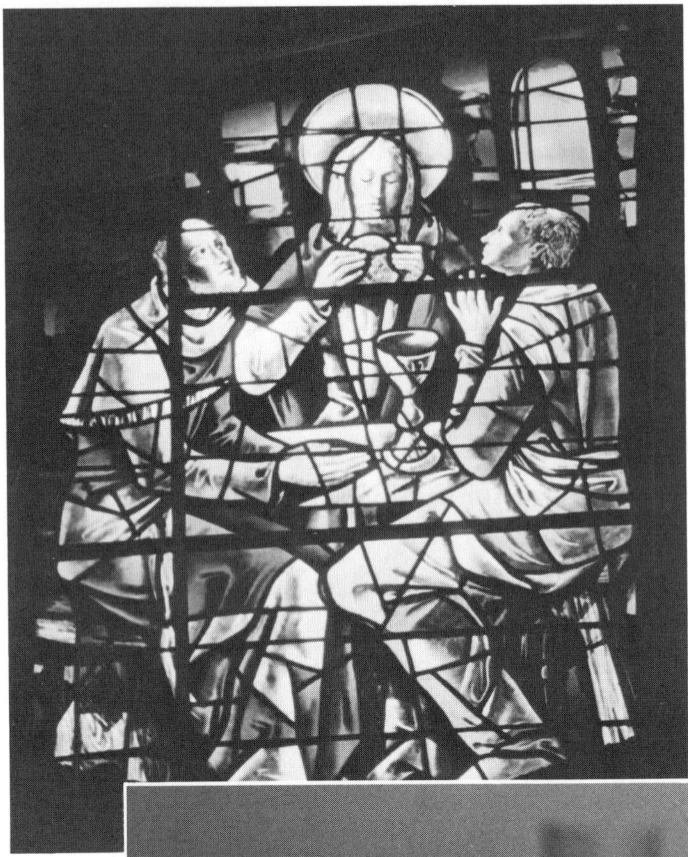
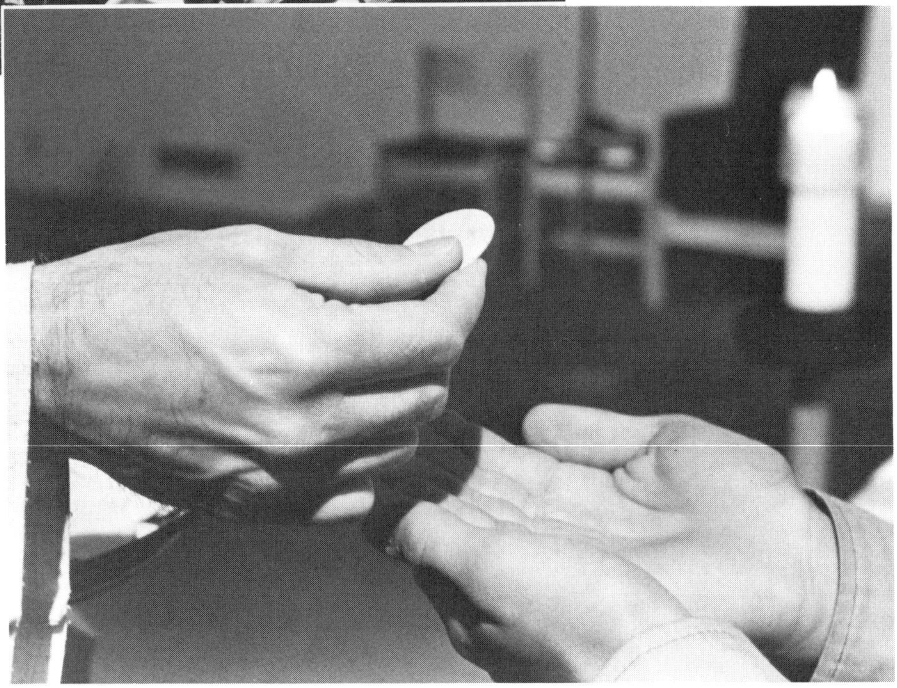

9 Receiving

The Road to Emmaus

(Luke 24:13-35)

**As the body of Christ
(the church community)
we are invited to receive the Lord's body
at the celebration of the Eucharist.**

REFLECTING

We Reflect on the Action of Jesus

In this story of the two men walking to Emmaus we discover how confused and fearful the friends of Jesus are following his death. Jesus joins the two men and offers comfort by explaining the scriptures to them. Finally, in the breaking of the bread, they recognize the Lord. The actions—took, blessed, broke, gave—performed in the setting of a meal powerfully recall to the two men other meals shared with Jesus. By these actions they recognize his presence.

There are liturgical overtones in this story. Jesus explained the scriptures and broke bread with the two men. These actions parallel the Liturgy of the Word and the Liturgy of the Eucharist in our celebration of Mass today. Early Christian celebrations in the home used these two parts.

The two men received Jesus' words. They invited him to walk with them, to share a meal with them, and they recognized him in the breaking of the bread. Jesus is always ready for us to receive him, to invite him into our lives. He comes to us in a special way in the breaking of the bread, the eucharistic meal. And through his word and through the breaking of the bread, Jesus receives us as his body. As the body of Christ we go forth, and like the two men we run with joy and tell the good news that Jesus is alive and with us.

We Reflect on the Action of Eucharist

The Eucharist is a sacrament of unity. The many grains of wheat that form the one bread speak clearly of how many may be one. As the church we, though many, are the one body of Christ. It is as the body of Christ that we are invited to receive the Lord's body. As we respond "Amen," we profess our belief in the real presence of Christ in the sacrament of the Eucharist (in the breaking of the bread) and in the people gathered. We receive the body of Christ and we are the body of Christ.

We Reflect on the Action of Family Living

Is there anything we have that we have not received from another? We are gifted, and our response to what we have received should be one of gratitude and thanksgiving. Saying yes to the gift of one another is the same yes we say to all people as the body of Christ. Receiving God's love and knowing we are lovable and capable of love, we offer our loving presence to our children. This presence becomes the foundation for their understanding of the real presence of Jesus in the eucharistic meal. Together as family we receive and recognize the presence of Jesus in the events of daily family living, in one another, in scripture and in the Eucharist.

EXPERIENCING

We Experience the Action of Jesus

A. Discuss the picture on page 75 with your child.

What are the three men doing? (resting, eating together, talking . . .)

Which one do you think is Jesus? (the one in the middle, the one breaking the bread . . .)

What is Jesus doing? (giving the others bread, breaking the bread, blessing the bread, holding the bread . . .)

Why do the two men look happy? (they like one another, they are enjoying the meal, they are glad to be with Jesus . . .)

What are they receiving from Jesus? (food, friendship, love . . .)

Do you remember a time that you received the same thing from someone you love? How did you feel?

B. Read the story to your child.

C. Pray the Prayer of Imagination at the end of the story.

D. Responding to the story: Remind your child that the words

"Jesus joined them"

come from the story you just read. Even though the two men are preoccupied, worried and sad, they are still courteous to a stranger. Give your child time to respond to the first statement on page 79. You might want to point out that Jesus comes to us in those we know—parents, brothers and sisters, relatives, friends—and in those who may be strangers to us—the poor, the sick, the lonely.

As your child shares the words or pictures he or she has chosen, introduce the theme of receiving. Everything we have and everything we are we have received from others. There are tangible gifts like food, clothing and toys, and intangible ones like joy, friendship and love. Life itself is a gift from God. The way we choose to respond to this gift and to the gifts of creation in our daily lives reflects our basic attitudes and values.

Ask your child:

How do you feel when you receive a gift?

How do you feel when someone says "I love you"?

Who shows you love by giving you food and clothes and a place to live?

Is there someone who helps you feel happy when you have been sad?

What is one gift you have received from God?

How do you feel about that gift?

How do you know that God loves you?

Can you name some of the people in your life who love you?

We show how we feel about a gift by our response. When the two men recognized Jesus, they were thankful and ran to tell others the good news. Talk about ways we show how much we appreciate a gift (saying thank you or writing thank-you notes, using the gift, giving a gift ourselves . . .). We want to express our thanks to Jesus when we daily welcome him into our lives. When we receive Jesus

The Road to Emmaus (Receiving)

in the Eucharist, we say thank you in our hearts.

Help your child write the thank-you prayer on page 79. Your child may want to say this prayer after receiving communion.

> *Optional:* Besides showing how we feel by what we say, we also show our gratitude for the gift of Jesus in the meal of the Eucharist by our actions.
> - Remind your child that in respect we fast for one hour before receiving the Eucharist.
> - Teach your child how to approach the table of the Lord with respect and reverence. Folded hands, for example, are a sign of reverence. Paying attention (not talking or looking around the church) shows respect.
> - Certain actions during the quiet time after receiving communion help us thank God and also show respect: kneeling, bowing the head, or assuming any position of reverence which allows us to reflect in silence.
> - Help your child recognize that we are the body of Christ. When we receive Jesus, we receive one another. Consider ways we can show respect to others (being courteous, caring, avoiding put-downs or gossip . . .).

As your child responds to the statements on page 80 under

"They recognized him in the breaking of the bread"

talk about the different ways Jesus is present to us: in the Eucharist, in his word (scripture), in other people, in the events of everyday living. You may want to mention to your child that Jesus is present in the actions we talk about in each chapter of this book: forgiving, celebrating, listening, caring, giving, sharing, remembering, belonging, receiving and serving. He is also present with us always and in a special way at communion.

Ask your child:

> *When did the two men finally recognize Jesus?* (when he broke the bread)
>
> *Do you remember another meal when Jesus took bread, blessed it, broke it and gave it to his friends?* (the Last

Supper, the night before he died, the Passover meal . . .)

At what meal do we do this today? (the eucharistic meal, the Mass . . .)

When do we listen to the word of God? (at Mass, when we hear the Bible stories . . .)

Who are some of the people who will break bread with you on your first communion day? (parents, brothers and sisters, relatives, friends, teachers, people in the parish . . .)

Your child may want his or her friends and relatives to sign their names on page 103 of the *Child's Book*.

E. Besides knowing that the bread of the Eucharist is different from ordinary bread, that it is the body of Christ, our children should show a genuine desire to receive Jesus. Talk with your child about your own desire to receive Jesus in the Eucharist. Then help your child write the prayer on page 81 telling Jesus how much he or she wants to receive him in communion.

We Experience the Action of Eucharist

A. Help your child complete the word AMEN on page 82.

B. Explain to your child that just as Christ at the Last Supper gave his body and blood to the apostles, so the priest or eucharistic minister presents the gift of the Eucharist to the people. The minister raises the bread of life before each communicant and says, "The body of Christ." The person answers, "Amen." For distribution from the cup, the minister says, "The blood of Christ." Again the response is "Amen." Communion is a gift of the Lord. Our Amen shows our gratitude and thanksgiving for all God has given us in Jesus.

Speak about your faith in Jesus as the bread of life. Explain that though we see a piece of bread or a cup of wine, we believe it is the Lord himself we receive, his body and blood. Remind your child that Jesus himself said the words that the priest says over the bread and wine: "This is my body. . . . This is my blood."

C. As a community, the body of Christ, we are invited to receive the Lord's body. Remind your child to say a quiet prayer as he or she prepares to receive communion, perhaps a simple phrase like "Jesus, I love you." Explain that we receive communion either kneeling or standing to show respect and reverence for the Eucharist. We can receive by having the minister place the bread of life on our tongue or

The Road to Emmaus (Receiving)

in our hand. We can receive by drinking from the cup. Remind your child to thank God after receiving communion for Jesus' gift of himself in the Eucharist and in the people gathered.

During Mass on Sunday, point out to your child the time of the COMMUNION RITE.

We Experience the Action of Family Living

A. Have your child share at a family meal the prayer he or she wrote (page 81).

B. During the meal, ask your child to tell in his or her own words the story of THE ROAD TO EMMAUS. Discuss ways we can recognize Jesus in family living. Plan how family members can make the first communion day a special one for your child. You might want to make a list of people to invite to the celebration. Making and sending the invitations could be a family project.

C. Place a sign for THE ROAD TO EMMAUS on the *Jesus Tree*.

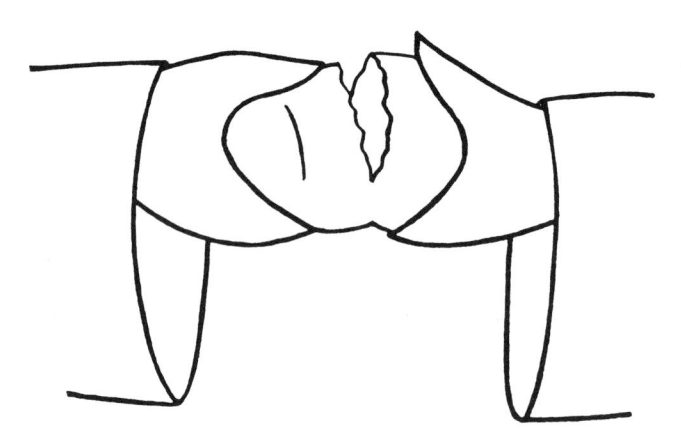

PRAYING AT OUR HOME TABLE OF THE LORD

Place a loaf of bread on the table. Light the family candle.

Leader: Lord, bread is a sign of our oneness.
You are the bread of life.
May we daily receive your life and love through the people gathered around this table of the Lord.
We offer this bread to you as a sign of our oneness as we say:

Hold the bread as all present say the blessing.

All: **Bless us, O Lord, and these your gifts which we are about to receive from your bounty through Christ our Lord. Amen.**

Leader: In the breaking of the bread, Lord, may we know you and one another.

Break the bread and pass it around to all the family members. When everyone has a piece of the bread, say:

All: **Amen.**

Eat the bread.

Leader: As a family let us sit in silence for a moment and thank God in our hearts for the gift of bread which gives us life and for the gift of love we share with one another.

Pause.

Let us thank each family member for the gift of love he or she has given us.

Allow time for family members to exchange expressions of thanks:

Each Person: _____*(Name)*_____, thank you for loving me.

The Road to Emmaus (Receiving)

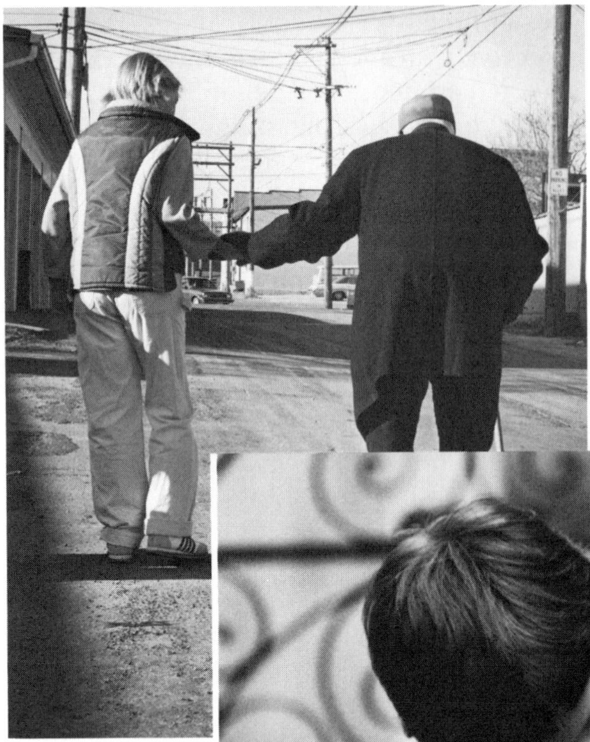

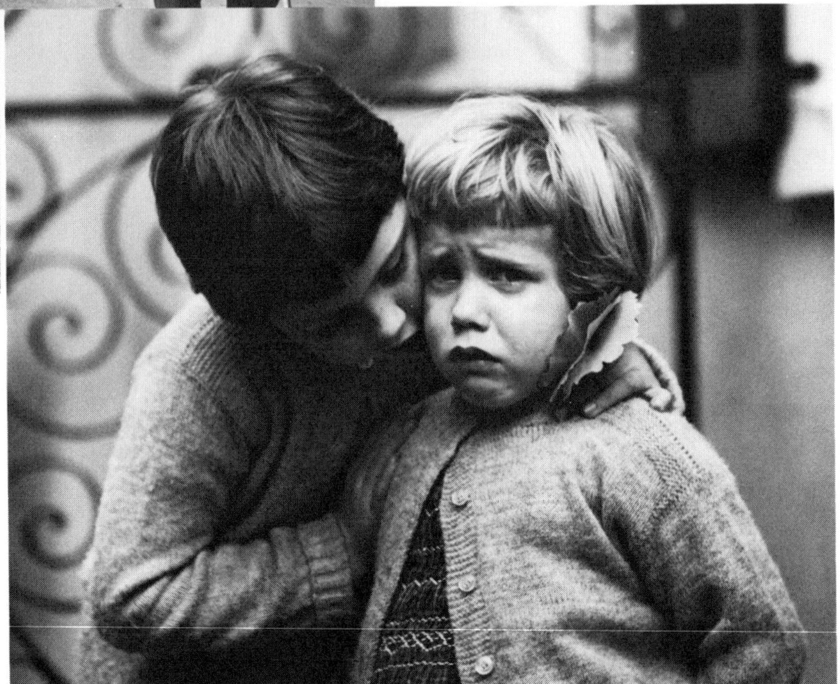

10 Serving

Jesus in Others

(Matthew 25:31-40)

When we live the life of the Eucharist, we serve Jesus in others.

REFLECTING

We Reflect on the Action of Jesus

There is no parallel in the other gospels for this imaginative scene in which Jesus presents the heart of his moral teachings. This is the source for the spiritual and corporal works of mercy.

Like the apostles, we want to know how to love and serve the Lord. Jesus has answered clearly: When we serve those in need, we are serving him. Jesus identifies himself with those in need, with the least important. Our behavior toward others, then, is our behavior toward God. Here we have the way to fulfill the great commandment of love—love God and love your neighbor—clearly spelled out. And we need never feel alone in our struggle to love and serve Jesus in others; as the family of God we have one another's support.

We Reflect on the Action of Eucharist

The effect of the Eucharist is love, love which leads to the service of others. We assemble as God's people, and in our oneness we are blessed. But the celebration of the Eucharist does not end with the last words of the liturgy. It continues as we go forth together as family to continue loving, celebrating and serving God in others. The Eucharist becomes the occasion and cause for a deeper commitment to the work of building the kingdom through love and service. Jesus invites us to come share the eucharistic meal with him and to come serve his people with him.

We Reflect on the Action of Family Living

In simple acts of loving kindness to one another, we continue the action of the Eucharist in our homes. We have already performed many of the works of love in our family; we have fed, clothed, comforted, and so on. But Jesus asks that we see him in the people who seem unimportant, those people that our world considers insignificant. As a family we need to awaken to ways that we can creatively and compassionately respond to the needs of others, especially to the "least" among our brothers and sisters.

EXPERIENCING

We Experience the Action of Jesus

A. Discuss the picture on page 83 with your child.

Where is Jesus? (with his friends, near the crowd . . .)

What do you think Jesus is saying? (help others, take care of the people . . .)

Do some of the people need help? How could you help them? (give them food, buy them clothes, talk with them, be friendly . . .)

Can you remember a time when you needed help?

Who helped you?

How?

B. Read the story to your child.

C. Pray the Prayer of Imagination at the end of the story.

D. Responding to the story: Remind your child that the words

"Jesus showed us how to serve those who are in need"

come from the story you just read. Give your child time to respond to the statements in this section. For the first statement, it may be helpful to use the signs on your *Jesus Tree* to help your child recall different stories about Jesus that you have read together. Jesus taught us how to treat others by the way he lived and the stories he told. Encourage your child to choose one of the stories about Jesus serving a person in need.

Ask your child:

How did Jesus know the person was in need?

How did Jesus help the person?

(The answers will depend on the story your child has chosen.)

Have you ever helped someone in need? How?

There are three steps in serving effectively: 1) recognizing a need; 2) considering how Jesus would have responded to the need; and 3) choosing a way to respond to the need. Your child will begin to grow in sensitivity and awareness through your recognition of and response to the needs of others. And when you praise other people who serve those in need, either people who serve in your local community or well-known examples like Mother Teresa, you hold out good models for your child to imitate.

As the family of God, we continue Jesus' work of bringing God's kingdom to all people by serving others. As your child responds to the statements on page 88 under

"I tell you, whenever you did this for one of the least important, you did it for me!"

share how you feel when someone tries to help you. This could be a good place to talk about a time when your child did something for you. Children are not always aware that they are able to bring help and services to adults. Also point out that it is not just how we feel in serving and helping others that is important. We must always be sensitive to the feelings and the dignity of those being served.

Ask your child:

Can you think of a time you felt good when someone helped you?

Can you think of a time you were helped but didn't feel very good about it? Why do you think you felt like that? (the person was bossy, didn't seem to really care, didn't listen to what I wanted, seemed to be in a hurry, made me feel dumb, blamed me for my problem . . .)

E. Help your child make the picture on page 89.

Jesus in Others *(Serving)*

> *Who are some of the people who are not considered very important in our world?* (the poor, the unloved, old people, handicapped people, lonely people, those who are always sick . . .)
>
> *How can we show love to Jesus by showing love to the people in our picture?* (Jesus is in each person, Jesus said we serve him when we serve them . . .)

This is a profound message. Just as we recognize Jesus in the meal of the Eucharist, so we now recognize him in the people we meet, especially in the people that our society looks down on. Even after the Sunday liturgy has ended, the action of the Eucharist continues as we love and serve Jesus in others.

Children in the primary grades are capable of concrete actions of serving and loving others. Discuss ways your son or daughter can put into action the response he or she gave to the second statement on page 88.

Or ask your child:

> *What could you do for someone who is sick?*
>
> *How could you help a family member?*
>
> *How could you welcome someone new in the neighborhood?*

You may want to continue to ask questions based on each of the six works of love mentioned in the story, or choose to talk about one of the works which is especially appropriate to the recent experiences of your child. Your child may be surprised by the works of love he or she is already doing for others.

We Experience the Action of Eucharist

A. Help your child complete the words GO IN PEACE TO LOVE AND SERVE THE LORD on page 90. These are the words the priest says at the Concluding Rite of the Mass.

B. Read all the words of the Concluding Rite on page 90. Explain that the word *amen* is given in response to the blessing the priest offers us. When we bless God, we give praise for the goodness and gifts of God. When we bless people, we ask that the goodness of God continue in each of us. The response *Thanks be to God* is an expression of joy. We have received the gift of Jesus in the Eucharist and now we want to share that gift by serving Jesus in others. We are eager to build God's kingdom of love.

C. With your child, choose one way to serve someone this week.

At the celebration of the Eucharist, point out the CONCLUDING RITE to your child. Note the gesture of the priest as he blesses us.

We Experience the Action of Family Living

A. Have your child share the picture of Jesus today (page 89) at a family meal. Discuss ways your family can help.

B. During the meal, ask your child to tell in his or her own words the story of JESUS IN OTHERS. As a family choose one of the ways you discussed above to continue Jesus' work of building the kingdom through love and service. Remember that in serving others, we serve Jesus. Or, the way your child chose to serve someone this week (see page 88) may be appropriate for the whole family. Be sure to thank your child for sharing.

Optional

A Service Project

This may be a helpful way of choosing a family service project. Fold a piece of paper into four squares. In the first square, write *family;* in the second, *school;* in the third, *friends;* and in the fourth, *world.* Under each heading write a need that you see or the name of someone you could help. Consider what Jesus would do in each situation. Now choose one need or person. Write your plan for serving. On a calendar mark your schedule for carrying out this family service project.

C. Place a sign (see next page) for JESUS IN OTHERS on the *Jesus Tree.*

Jesus in Others *(Serving)*

PRAYING AT OUR HOME TABLE OF THE LORD

Use your tablecloth for the home table of the Lord for this meal. You may want to draw signs of service to others on the cloth.

Leader: Lord,
we know you in the meal of the Eucharist,
and in the people gathered to celebrate the meal.
You send us forth to know you
    in the people we meet every day,
    in our family,
    in our friends,
    in the world.
In serving them, we serve you.

In the silence of our hearts,
we think about your words, Lord:
    "Whenever you did this for one of the
    least important, you did it for me!"

Pause.

And now we give our hands, Lord.
With these hands we want to do your work.
We want to bring your kingdom to all people.

Make the sign of the cross in the palm of each family member as you say:

_____*(Name)*_____, go forth to love and serve God in others.

Let us now bow our head for God's blessing:

> In the name of the Father
> and of the Son,
> and of the Holy Spirit.

All: **Amen.**

Jesus in Others *(Serving)* 95

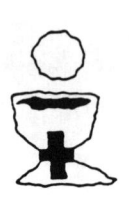